Mathemagica

Music

Production

Second Edition

By Derrick Scott van Heerden

Contents

Introduction

This book is the result of more than 10 years of research and practical experimentation that I have done into the world of sound, its connection to the universe and its effects on people. To do this this properly I moved out of the city and into the countryside, leaving my band and DJ career so that I could work undisturbed and uninfluenced by social matters. I spent weeks, months and eventually years either out in nature thinking or isolated in my workroom, reading a lot, trying many sonic experiments and drawing many charts full of frequencies and ratios.

Using this time well, I designed a system where all aspects of my music were in harmony with each other, the bpm of my track, the frequencies of all the notes in my scale, the effects, the types of melodies used, and all other aspects of my sound. I also learned how to embed various brainwave entrainment frequencies such as binaural beats, isochronic tones and even subliminal sounds, into this music in ways that were harmonious and in time / tune with the music itself, without disturbing the sound at all, instead using it as a resonator to make them even more powerful. The human brain mirrors any sounds that enter the ears, so having all of the beats and sounds in mathematical / musical harmony with each other is the best way to get powerful effects from your music.

While learning to do all of this I had to do quite a bit of mathematical calculation, dividing and multiplying of frequencies. After doing this for some time I noticed that certain numbers would appear over and over again because they were more useful and easy to work with than others. These numbers could be divided or multiplied in many ways while still staying nice and whole, not spawning too many decimals and confusion. Soon I had a collection of these useful numbers that were the best for all kinds of mathematical calculations. I called them "magic numbers". When I looked closer at them I found that they mirrored many interesting things like the orbits and sizes of the Sun, Earth, Moon, the golden ratio, sacred geometry, the platonic solids, the light spectrum, and most importantly each other.

In this book you will find lots of information about these matters, but most importantly you will find tutorials that teach you how to do everything that I have learned in your own studio. So, if you really want to apply the hermetic "as above – so below" maxim to your music, then this is the book for you!

How sound works

Sound is a vibration that travels away from its source in all directions as air pressure waves, almost like bubbles or "spheres" that are inside each other. When we look at sound waves on a computer they don't look like bubbles, though. They look like two dimensional waves showing you how many are being produced over a certain amount of time. The two images below are of a sine wave which is the only sound wave that has this perfectly smooth curve.

Sine waves

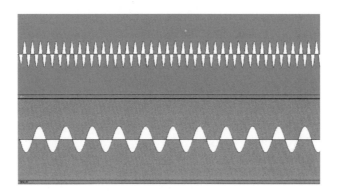

The high-pitched sound above has a higher vibration and many small waves, while the lower bass sound below it has a lower vibration and makes less waves over the same amount of time. Your speakers also vibrate according to this wave. When the wave is at the top, your speaker is pushed forward. When the wave is at the bottom, your speaker is sucked in. And when it's in the middle, so is the speaker. The same thing is true for a drum skin or tuning fork, as it is the vibration of the object producing the sound that makes the air vibrate in waves that then move away in all directions and make other objects like your ear drums and body vibrate.

What does Hz mean?

To measure the frequency of sound waves we need to use numbers. The standard way to measure sound waves is in cycles per second. The term used for this is Hertz or Hz. This means that if you hit a 512 Hz tuned tuning fork or play a 512 Hz tone on a speaker, they will vibrate exactly 512 times in one second and will also make 512 air pressure waves per second.

Harmonics

If you look at the sound waves of different musical instruments on a computer you will see that each one has a waveform that looks different. Middle C on trumpet will have the same amount of waves over the same amount of time as middle C on a piano, but the waves themselves will be a slightly different shape.

Trumpet and Piano

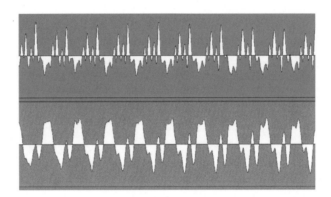

So, what is it that makes these sound waves have different shapes? The very simple and amazing fact that all musical sounds are actually made from various combinations of pure sine waves; more specifically they are made from one single "fundamental" sine wave and then many smaller/higher sine waves called harmonics or overtones, all mixed together to make a new sound wave. Whenever two or more sine waves are played at the same time, their sound waves interact with each other to produce a different and more complex sound wave. This only works with sine waves because they are the only type of sound that has no harmonics of its own. Although all musical sounds are made from sine waves in various combinations, they almost never occur as single waves in nature or musical instruments.

There is another way to view sounds on a computer, and that is by using a spectrum analyzer. You can download the same spectrum analyzer used in the following images (Voxengo Span®) for free at this link http://www.voxengo.com/product/span/. With a spectrum analyzer you can see all the harmonics in a sound instead of just the waveform. In the next image you can see the spectrum analyzer view of a pure sine wave from a synthesizer playing middle C:

Pure sine wave (middle C)

Now let's look again at the sounds of the piano and the trumpet also playing middle C, but this time through the spectrum analyzer:

Piano

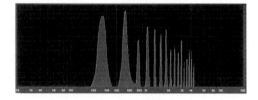

Trumpet

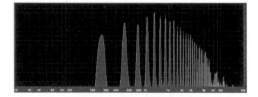

As you can see, the trumpet and the piano both have that same fundamental C sine wave on the left, while to the right of it you can see the rest of harmonics. In both sounds they have the same-sized intervals or gaps between them, only their volumes are different. It is these variations in the volumes of the harmonics that make a piano sound like a piano and a trumpet like a trumpet.

The same applies to almost all pleasing musical sounds, digital and acoustic.

Digital saw tooth wave

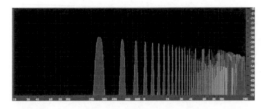

Acoustic flute

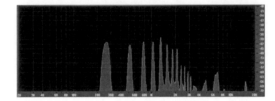

Digital string

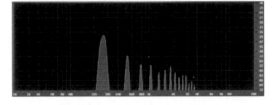

Human voice

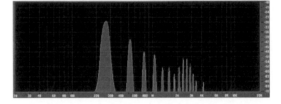

You can actually tell what a sound will sound like by looking at its harmonics. If the fundamental and lower harmonics up to the sixth are the loudest, then the sound will be rich and warm. If, however, the seventh and harmonics above it are louder, the tone will be more harsh and metallic. These days we can just pass a sound through a low pass filter or EQ to reduce the higher harmonics, whereas before all instruments had to be built taking this into account.

There are instances, such as with over-stressed strings, where the harmonic series gets "stretched" slightly, or with certain metallic instruments where the overtones behave in a completely different way. Such instruments often have their own traditional scales that mirror these strange harmonics, a good example being traditional Indonesian music.

Indonesian gamelan

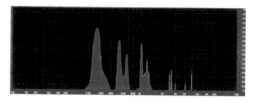

Metal xylophone from Java

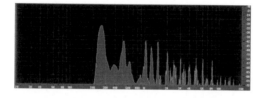

Church bell

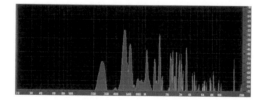

For most of the sounds used in modern day music, however, the harmonics will follow the same pattern as sounds like piano, flute or the human voice do. If you want to hear the harmonics in any sound as a melody, just play it through a bell EQ and sweep the frequency up and down.

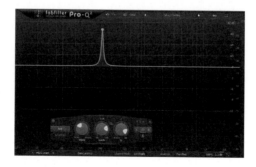

These natural intervals are known as the harmonic series. Another way to look at the harmonic series is by dividing a piece of string into the even parts seen in the following image. It only shows the first 7 harmonics but the pattern repeats infinitely, or until the acoustic limitations of the instrument playing it are met. These are the same intervals as seen in the spectrum analyzer pictures of sounds like the piano, flute or human voice, getting closer and closer together as you go higher up the spectrum.

Harmonic strings

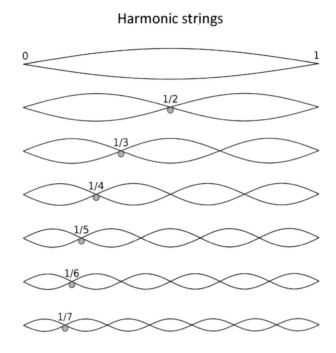

Any sound can actually be modeled by playing many different synthesized sine waves arranged in the same way as the original sound. This is how many digital synths work, recreating piano and other sounds using only sine waves. This type of synthesis is actually quite simple, since you only need to adjust the volume of each harmonic to recreate just about any musical sound. Despite the fact that the synthesized piano will sound like a piano, it will obviously never sound as authentic as a real piano. There definitely is some magic in real harmonics that is not present in synthesized ones. You can prove this by taking any digital or VST synthesizer and pushing the resonance on your main filter to full. If you now do a filter sweep through the resonance-enhanced harmonics of your sound, it will not make a nice sound. It is more likely to be a less than pleasing sound which may even hurt your ears. But try the same thing with a 100% analogue Korg ms-20 or Moog, and you will get lovely smooth tones similar to whale sounds.

This must be because the analogue synth actually generates harmonics naturally, while the digital synth tries to model those using numbers. This must also be the reason why real tube amplifiers sound so pleasing, and why "cutting" frequencies sounds better than boosting with digital equipment, while with analogue equipment you can boost frequencies all you want.

The harmonic series is also what you hear in overtone chanting, where the singer learns to use their mouth as an EQ to boost each overtone individually and play a melody with them. The sound of a monochord, Bushman bow, jaw harp and the bugle also use these same harmonic intervals as melodies. If you hear these intervals as a melody they sound very familiar and comforting. The bugle is in fact an amazing instrument. It is like a brass trumpet but it has no valves or keys, so you can only change notes by blowing harder or softer into the mouth piece. The result of this is that the bugle can only play the notes of the harmonic series in their natural order and no other notes. So, if your bugle is tuned to C then the notes it will play will be C, C1, G1, C2, E2, and G2 (harmonic series), although most bugles are made so that they can't play the first C, and can't play higher than the sixth harmonic (G2).

Intervals in relation to the fundamental with bugle tones in green:

Harmonic	Note	Interval
1	C	Fundamental
2	C	Octave
3	G	Octave + perfect fifth
4	C	Two octaves
5	E	Two octaves + major third
6	G	Two octaves + perfect fifth
7	?	Two octaves + harmonic seventh

Intervals between each harmonic with bugle tones in green:

1	C	
		Octave
2	C	
		Perfect fifth
3	G	
		Perfect fourth
4	C	
		Major third
5	E	
		Minor third
6	G	
		Septimal minor third
7	?	

With the exception of the octave, which is perfect in most instruments, the sizes of these intervals are slightly different to those of the same names on a piano or most other modern day instruments. The modern day intervals are based on, and are close estimates of, these original harmonic intervals, though. The reason why the bugle only goes up to the sixth harmonic is because the septimal minor third between harmonics 6 and 7 is basically a very flat minor third and sounds quite dissonant, which is also why there is no interval based on it in the modern day equal temperament scale.

If you go higher up the series, you will find a major whole tone that is very similar to the major whole tone in the standard equal temperament scale between harmonics 8 and 9. Above that the intervals get even smaller, with a nice semi-tone to be found between harmonics 15 and 16. Above that the intervals get smaller than anything found in our modern day scale. Eventually they get so small that you can no longer hear the difference between consecutive harmonics, and playing through them just sounds like a sweeping tone.

Anything that oscillates or vibrates has a fundamental frequency and therefore harmonics, too. Sound, light, certain tiny particles, planetary orbits, alternating electric currents and rotating machines are all in a state of vibration. This is why you find these same harmonics intervals playing important roles in many seemingly unrelated fields such as sound healing, subatomic particle science, astronomy and industrial energy grid optimization. The harmonic series is even the basis of Zip's law, but that is another story...

As a number sequence the harmonic series is very simple. If you start with 1 it will be 1, 2, 3, 4, 5, 6, 7, 8, 9, 10, 11, 12, 13, 14, 15 etc. Here is how you calculate the harmonic series of any number; I will use 9 Hz for an example. Octaves of 9 Hz are usually associated with the note D because they are very close to D in 440 Hz based equal temperament, so this chart starts with 9 Hz as D. (some of the note names above the sixth harmonic are not very accurate when compared to equal temperament, and are just there are a guide).

Sum	Frequency	Number	Note
9 x 1 =	09 Hz	1st Harmonic	D
9 x 2 =	18 Hz	2nd Harmonic	D
9 x 3 =	27 Hz	3rd Harmonic	A
9 x 4 =	36 Hz	4th Harmonic	D
9 x 5 =	45 Hz	5th Harmonic	F#
9 x 6 =	54 Hz	6th Harmonic	A
9 x 7 =	63 Hz	7th Harmonic	C
9 x 8 =	72 Hz	8th Harmonic	D
9 x 9 =	81 Hz	9th Harmonic	E
9 x 10 =	90 Hz	10th Harmonic	F#

Another way to calculate the harmonic series is to add the first number to itself, and then to keep adding it to your answer over and over again. So, for 9 it would simply be 9+9=18, 18+9=27, 27+9=36...

When you use certain numbers (like 9) to start the harmonic series, some amazing anomalies occur. If, for example, you look at the "frequency" column in the above image, you will see that the first number of each successive Hz frequency is 0, 1, 2, 3, 4, 5, 6, 7, 8, 9 going downwards, and that the second number in each does the same thing going upwards. You can also add the two digits in any of them together and they will always add up to 9 (0+9=9, 1+8=9, 2+7=9 etc.) Although this particular anomaly only happens when the harmonic series is started with 9, using other numbers will still produce interesting patterns.

In any series of numbers, each number can also be referred to by its sequence number. This number is the point in the sequence where that number occurs. If, for example, you have the sequence 9 - 18 - 27 - 36 - 45, then 9 has a sequence number of 1; 18 has a sequence number of 2; 27 has 3 and so on. It does not matter what number you start the harmonic series with. The first harmonic (fundamental) will always have a sequence number of 1, the second harmonic will always have a sequence number of 2, and the third harmonic will have 3 and so on. Because the sequence numbers for the harmonic series are exactly the same as its frequencies when it is started with 1 Hz, you can learn a lot about the connections between vibration and numbers by studying them. What you learn can then be applied to the harmonic series when it is started with any number or frequency, as the intervals will always be the same.

The octave

The word octave is derived from the word "octa-" which means "having 8". This came from the early observation that the octave seems to like being divided into 7 unequal parts, with the eighth being the octave of the first. The 7 tone major scale and the 7 colors in the rainbow are good examples of this. All of the scales in this book repeat over octaves, which is why the charts showing them only ever cover one octave.

The octave is the second harmonic in the harmonic series. If you make a guitar string exactly half its length it will play the same note but one octave higher, and if you play middle C on a piano then its octave will be the next C on the piano. This is actually the only perfect harmonic interval in the normal equal temperament scale; all of the other intervals are just close estimates. If you are working with rhythms then an octave higher will be the same beat, but exactly twice the speed. The octave is the most common rhythm in all music, and musically it is the most harmonious interval. You can find it in the opening interval of the songs "singing in the rain" and "somewhere over the rainbow".

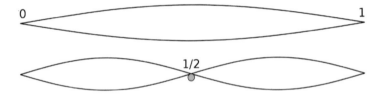

An octave in mathematics is any number doubled or halved (multiplied or divided by 2). You can go upward or downward forever with octaves, there is always another number twice as big or half the size of the number you have.

In the harmonic series, each harmonic actually repeats over octaves as you go up it. In the following image of the first 31 harmonics, I have color-coded repeating octaves and arranged them side by side making this easy to see.

There is a law called the "law of octaves" used in various other scientific and esoteric fields. It states that when a vibration is doubled of halved in frequency, the new frequency will have very similar properties to the first frequency. This is why C on a piano has very similar sonic properties to the next C and all other C's on the piano, while it has less similar properties to the rest of the notes in-between. The fact that all C's are called C and don't have different names makes it easy to understand just how similar the properties of octaves are to each other.

This explains how, while working with sound frequencies and music, you can freely multiply or divide a frequency by 2 any number of times, doubling or halving it in octaves to get higher or lower frequencies that will always have very similar properties and be in perfect harmony with the original frequency (something that is done a lot in this book and frequency work in general). It is important to remember that octaves are not exactly the same, only very similar. It is also true in mathematics; while the numbers 1, 2, 4, 8, 16 etc. are obviously not the same number, they do also have similar properties when used in mathematical calculations.

The octave is the basis for many important things. For example, when human life starts it starts as a single cell which then divides into 2, then 4, then 8, 16, 32 and 64 (after 64 skin, hair and other cells start to form). It is also used for many things in the digital realm, 32 / 64 bit processors, 512 / 1024 / 2048 MB RAM or flash memory. Minecraft blocks and many other digital things rely on the number sequence: 1-2-4-8-16-32-64-128-256-512-1024-2048-4096...

Brainwave entrainment

Entrainment is the name used when a sound affects an object, be it a human brain, a bit of fluff stuck to a speaker, an opera singer breaking a glass with sound, a scientist using acoustic levitation to levitate a drop of water, or even shrimps creating light from sound using sonoluminescense.

Sound does not only have an effect your mind, it also affects your body. If you turn your speakers up loud enough you will feel it for yourself. It is a fact that listening to fast music will make you exited, while listening to slow music will have a relaxing effect. This works on all levels affecting your brainwaves, heart rate and blood pressure. It is actually a lot more specific than just feeling relaxed or excited, though. Listening to a drum beat at 135 bpm, for example, will eventually entrain your brainwaves to exactly 135 bpm, which will put you into a nice trance. Because all sounds are vibrations it is really true that all sounds, both rhythms and tones, will have entraining effects. Beats on a drum and a smooth audio tone are actually very similar, depending on how close you zoom into the waveform. So, even a high-pitched tone like 288 Hz will still create some form of entrainment even at this high frequency.

Brainwave theory

If you want to learn more about how sound affects the mind, brainwave theory is a good scientific place to start. This is because scientists have mapped out our brainwaves using EEG machines, and they have tested audio frequencies on people while they are connected to these machines. In doing this they have proven that our brainwaves adjust themselves to the same frequencies as sounds played into our ears, and that our brainwaves are divided into different states.

Brainwave theory has been known to shaman for thousands of years. All around the world they tend to beat their drums or rattles at about 4 beats per second (4 Hz) to induce shamanic trance states. EEG Tests have been done on people while they were under the influence of various hallucinogens such as Peyote, Ayahuasca and Mushrooms in shamanic situations and also while lucid dreaming. In most cases spikes in the theta range were observed, proving that the theta range (4Hz-8Hz) is indeed the correct frequency for shamanic or psychedelic work.

There are many charts online that differ on the exact range of each state and the amount of states, but in most of them each state covers approximately one octave. So, I have designed my own chart based on all of the charts that I have seen, but in my chart each state covers exactly one octave, giving me 7 different states that are pretty much the same as 90% of the brainwave charts I have seen. Some charts have the eighth state (high gamma) and some don't. This is because high gamma is above the normal rhythmic brainwave frequency range and starts around the point where rhythms come into the range of low bass audio (64 Hz = typical didgeridoo range). Obviously the exact point of crossover from rhythmic to tonal sound varies slightly from person to person, but it is always near the start of the "high gamma" octave. It is interesting to note that the same thing happens with light, which is why old 60 Hz refresh rate PC monitors and 60 Hz fluorescent lights caused headaches while 75 Hz did not.

Brainwave states		
8 High gamma	64 - 128 Hz	Self-awareness, unity, super-conscious, deep insight, healing.
7 Gamma	32 - 64 Hz	Highly alert, insight, information processing, hyperactivity.
6 Beta	16 - 32 Hz	Alert, normal waking state, concentration, critical thought.
5 Alpha	8 - 16 Hz	Calm, daydreaming, visualization, memory, serotonin release.
4 Theta	4 - 8 Hz	Lucid dreaming, hallucinogenic state, intuition.
3 Delta	2 – 4 Hz	Transcendental meditation, sleep, natural opiate release.
2 Low delta	1 – 2 Hz	Deep meditation, deep sleep, endorphin release, healing.
1 Epsilon	0 – 1 Hz	Insight, self-awareness, unity, universal mind, deep healing.

It is important to remember that your brain does not just produce one state at a time; it produces more than one at the same time but in different amounts. So, in deep meditation you may have a spike in the theta or delta range, but you may still have a low level of alpha or beta waves present, keeping you awake and conscious at the same time. This is why it is good to use octaves like 2 Hz, 4 Hz and 8 Hz when you generate more than one brainwave frequency at the same time, because then each one will fall into a different brainwave state but will still be in harmony with the others.

If you look at the brainwave chart above, you can see that as you move upward through the rhythmic brainwave states they get faster, making you more alert, awake and even a bit stressed when you get to the fast drum roll type rhythms of beta and gamma. When you get to high gamma they become a smooth bass tone, which has a similar effect on your brainwaves as the very slow epsilon rhythms. This is quite interesting as the properties of the brainwave states seem to have done a full circle after 8 octaves, although it is more like a spiral because epsilon and high gamma may have more similar properties to each other than to the states in-between. But they are definitely not exactly the same.

In the following chart the red-colored horizontal rows are separated by 8 octaves. This first red row starts with 0 Hz, the point where rhythms start. The second one is where rhythm changes over to smooth bass audio. The top one ends near to the end of the average person's hearing range (super humans can hear up to 20000 Hz). So, it would seem like interesting things tend to happen every 8 octaves.

Audio	8192 Hz to 16384 Hz
Audio	4096 Hz to 8192 Hz
Audio	2048 Hz to 4096 Hz
Audio	1024 HZ to 2048 Hz
Audio	512 Hz to 1024
Audio	256 Hz to 512 Hz
Audio	128 Hz to 256 Hz
High gamma = 1/128 bass audio	64 Hz to 128 Hz
Gamma = 1/64 rhythm / very low bass	32 Hz to 64 Hz
Beta = 1/32 rhythm	16 Hz to 32 Hz
Alpha = 1/16 rhythm	8 Hz to 16 Hz
Theta = 1/8 rhythm	4 Hz to 8 Hz
Delta = 1/4 rhythm	2 Hz to 4 Hz
Low delta = 1/2 rhythm	1 Hz to 2 Hz
Epsilon = 1/1 rhythm	0 Hz to 1 Hz

Keep this in mind when you read later chapters in which the octave is divided into 7 parts to make a major scale, with the eighth part (octave) having very similar properties to the first.

The three most commonly used methods for inducing brainwave entrainment using sound today are binaural beats, monaural beats and isochronic tones.

Binaural beats

The way binaural beats work is simple. Using headphones or carefully placed speakers, you play an audio tone into one of your ears while, at the same time, playing the same audio tone but at a slightly lower or higher frequency into your other ear. Listening to this audio will entrain your brainwaves to the frequency that is the difference between the frequencies of the two slightly different tones. So, if you play 100 Hz tone into one ear and a 108 Hz tone into the other, the resulting tone will entrain your brainwaves to 8 Hz (alpha brainwaves). If you actually listen to this you will hear a tone panning left and right 8 times a second. If, however, you listen to just one of the tones on its own by switching off one of your speakers or removing one side of your headphones, you will hear just a smooth 100 Hz tone on one side and a 108 Hz tone on the other. For some reason listening to them together creates a tone that pans from left to right, but has a fairly stable sounding pitch that averages the two frequencies. So, in the end 100 Hz with 108 Hz will sound like a 104 Hz tone that wobbles 8 in times a second. Obviously if the tones are very far apart it will become a chord, which is why most brainwave charts don't go much higher than 40 Hz.

It is important to remember that the de-tune wobble speed and the averaged tone are both going to have entraining effects. This is why it will be best if the tone is in harmony with the main brainwave frequency or de-tune wobble speed. The law of octaves is obviously a good thing to use here. So, if you want an audio tone that is in tune / harmony with 8 Hz, just double or multiply 8 Hz by 2 a few times to get higher octaves that are within hearing range, and so can be used as audio tones. In this case 64 Hz, 128 Hz and 256 Hz will be good frequencies to use for tones as they are perfect octaves of 8 Hz. To split them for 8 Hz binaural beats, just calculate what frequencies are 4 Hz above and below your frequency. So, for 128 Hz you will play a 124 Hz and a 132 Hz tone together, then you will hear a 128 Hz tone with an 8 Hz wobble speed. You can also use other harmonic intervals instead of octaves for this, but octaves are the best place to start.

Apart from entraining your brainwaves to a specific frequency, binaural beats also have the effect of synchronizing your left - right brain hemispheres so that they fire in a left - right sequence, and so are in better harmony with each other. I am sure this could increase the efficiency of your brain by interleaving your thought processes more evenly; a bit like dual channel RAM. It is worth noting that you can get a very similar and equally powerful effect by simply panning a tone single left and right using auto pan. I actually prefer this method because there is no de-tuning involved.

Monaural beats

Monaural beats are just binaural beats that are played in mono instead of stereo, and so can be played on any speaker arrangement. When you listen to them you will hear a tone with its volume rising and falling at your de-tune frequency. They do entrain your brainwaves just like any modulated or rhythmic sound does, which is why you can mimic there effects very well by using a timed tremolo effect (amplitude modulation) on a single sine wave.

Binaural and monaural beats are most accurate when you use pure sine waves as audio tones. This is because a sine wave is the only sound that has no harmonics or overtones of its own (overtones will stimulate other brainwave frequencies), and so it is the best sound to use for accurate work where you only want to stimulate one frequency at a time. It is true, however, that any carrier frequency will still have a strong entraining effect. Musical sounds may even be better than pure tones, because the human brain is not used to only generating one fixed non-modulating frequency at a time. Using sounds which are rich in overtones, especially natural sounds with their slight modulations, may be better for you as your brain is used to processing this more natural type of sound. It is a fact that binaural beats have been used safely for centuries in this way; for example, Tibetans using 2 or more de-tuned Tibetan bowls or Aborigines using de-tuned didgeridoos.

Isochronic tones

Isochronic tones are often sold as some new technology, even though they too have been used for thousands of years. All an isochronic tone actually consists of is just a repeating pulse of sound, like a machine going "beep beep beep" at a specific amount of beeps per second (Hz).

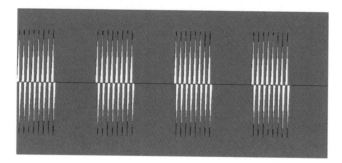

To make an isochronic tone 100% accurate, meaning that a 4 Hz pulse (4 beeps per second) will entrain your brainwaves to exactly 4 Hz, the gaps between the tones need to be exactly the same length as the tones themselves. It is also best to use pure sine waves for accurate Hz work although any sound, even drums, will still work very well.

If you are using tuned tones, it is best if the tone is set to a frequency that is in harmony with the speed at which it is pulsing on and off. Then both will work together instead of against each other. This is easy to do using the law of octaves as I have illustrated before. For example, if you want a frequency for an audio tone that is in harmony with a 4 Hz pulse or beat, you just multiply it by 2 a few times (octaves) until you get a frequency in the range that you want. When you do this, the amount of peaks in the waveform of each tone will always be an octave of the original frequency, as in the above image of a 4 Hz pulse which has 8 peaks in each pulse.

It takes up to 20 minutes for any brainwave entrainment to take full effect. So, because your brain is in a beta or alpha state most of the time, it makes sense to start your program around there and then slowly sweep the pitch to the frequency that you want to end up in. This gives your brainwaves time to adjust to the new frequencies. With binaural beats a very interesting program is to start in beta or alpha, then to sweep down to theta and hold the frequency there for some meditation time. From there you could go deeper down to delta for even deeper meditation, maybe even mix in some soft alpha waves or even some bird sounds at this point to stop you from falling asleep. If you are brave you can approach the no brain waves frequency of 0 Hz right at the bottom of the epsilon state. Then your 2 audio tones will no longer be de-tuned and will play the same note. I call this the "flat line" and have had out of body experiences at this point (only after the full 20 minute journey).

I find all of this very interesting; as you slowly lower your brainwave frequencies you go from a normal awake state to deeper levels of your mind. But then, as you go to the deepest levels where your brainwaves almost stop altogether, you can find yourself outside your body and fully "awake". Now you are in a state more similar to high gamma than the deep dreamless sleep associated with epsilon, only you are in another dimension. In fact, if you had set your carrier tone to a nice bass drone of 64 Hz like I did, then you should now be in the high gamma state and not epsilon at all. Suddenly this full circle of properties makes sense, how the highest and lowest brainwave states can be so similar even though they "should" be so different. As I mentioned before, it is more like a spiral as the properties of high gamma and epsilon are similar but not exactly the same.

Binaural beats, monoaural beats and isochronic tones are easy to make on a computer, alone or embedded into music. But I will explain that in a later chapter on practical applications of brainwave theory.

Traditional African entrainment methods

Although this all sounds very cutting edge, it has actually all been done before and is really ancient knowledge that we are just starting to re-learn now. I know from first-hand meetings with African healers that many African tribes have been using brainwave entrainment for centuries, inducing trance states with specific goals like healing disease or traveling to other worlds. When I asked them where they learned this science they mostly said that beings came from the sky in strange machines, and these beings then showed them how to make instruments like marimbas and mbiras, and also showed them how to play all their traditional, ritual and entrainment music. It sounds crazy but this is what they say, even tribes far away from each other that have never met.

The Dogon are a good example of this. They say that their alien friends came from Sirius, which incidentally was also a very important constellation to the ancient Egyptians. This is believable because they knew about Sirius B long before Westerners ever even knew it was there (it is not visible to the naked eye.) The Dogon clearly state that these beings taught them how to play music and also taught them agriculture and everything else that defines their culture. I know this is not only the case with Africans; it is also true with Native Americans and probably many other people around the world. But I live in Africa and prefer to learn from real experience, so I know more about Africans than other tribes.

There is one method used by many tribes here that I find to be very interesting:

They sit one person down on a mat and then have 2 mbira (thumb piano) players who sit each side of this person holding a mbira near each ear. They then play a special interlocking harmonic melody between the two players, in which each successive note enters the left then right ears, creating intense brainwave entrainment. This is easy to replicate with music software using two channels panned left and right, or a single one with tempo-synced auto pan.

Some tribes also work with very specific tempos. I have heard of shaman who spent years teaching a pupil to play one simple beat at a very specific speed. They say it can take a lifetime before the teacher says the beat is correct, and that some die of old age without ever getting it right. It is amazing because this beat sounds like the most basic bongo beat when listened to by somebody who is not familiar with this training.

Another thing that is done all over Africa is to play music using polyrhythms. These are identical to the harmonic series but expressed as rhythms. The first part / loop has 1 beat per loop. The next has 2 (in the same space of time); the next has 3, then 4 and so on. Obviously they play more complex rhythms based on these numbers and not just the single beats.

I have seen Bushmen do this in their trance dance. The women were singing and playing 4/4 rhythms on shakers and with hand claps, then the shaman joined in with rattles on his ankles, dancing / playing 3 or 6 beats over the women's 4 creating triplets. Sometimes he went deeper into trance and changed to other ratios / polyrhythms from the harmonic series like 5/4. The Bushmen also play other instruments like the single string Bushman bow. This instrument only plays the harmonics of the overtone series just like a monochord, but uses your mouth as a variable pitch resonator. The Bushmen are very tuned-in people. Their shaman are reputed to be the most powerful in all of Africa, and can basically see disease with "x-ray" vision and can fix it with their hands. It has been said by some that the Bushmen are the oldest race on Earth, so they really may be the wisest, too.

Another very common theme throughout Africa is to sing a repeating melody and then to raise the frequency a bit higher at the start of each loop. This could have the effect of raising your vibration to a higher level. It certainly does make me feel amazing.

Some tribes higher up in Africa also eat the powerful hallucinogen "IBOGA" before a trance quest. To join their cult you have to take a massive dose of this plant in order to "open the head" and meet with the spirit, "Bwiti", before gaining acceptance. They say that once you have accomplished this you automatically become a shaman. A friend of mine traveled very deep into this land and said he found whole villages occupied entirely by people who were such shaman. It is not only African shaman who do these types of things, there are shaman all over the world who use sound and plants for entering a trance. Good examples are the Native American peyote churches and the San Pedro, Ayahuasca, and mushroom shaman of South America.

Every culture on Earth actually has shaman. They are a type of person that can get born or reincarnated anywhere from the jungle to the city and back again. Such people usually work with two things: sound and plants. If you want to learn more about the plants / alchemy side of this, I highly recommend reading "Swim's Psychedelic Cook Book" (find it on Amazon).

Harmonic bpm

To apply brainwave theory to full music production, the next logical step would be to adjust the tempo of your music so that it is in harmony with your bass-line / reference pitch. If you do this then everything that uses your quantize, including tempo synched effects, will be in harmony with this frequency. This is a very good way to make music that has powerful effects, as your brainwaves will mirror this vibrational unity. It can also expand your production skills, because now the "tones" produced by modulating or slicing audio with high quantize settings like 1/64 will be perfectly in-tune with your bass-line.

The only problem is that your music workstation measures tempo in bpm (beats per minute), and audio frequency in Hz (beats / cycles per second). It is easy, however, to match Hz frequencies with bpm frequencies. I call this "harmonic bpm" and I have a very easy way of explaining how it works. The best example to start with is 1 Hz. A clock ticks once every second, so a clock could also be said to tick at 1 Hz.

We already know how to get the harmonic 256 Hz middle C that fits with 1 Hz using octaves, so now what we need is a bpm that is in harmony with 1 Hz and its octaves. This is very easy to work out because there are exactly 60 seconds in a minute. So, all you have to do is multiply 1 Hz by 60 and then we get our answer: 60 bpm. So, 1 Hz and 60 bpm are exactly the same frequency, as are 2 Hz and 120 bpm (2 x 60 = 120), 4 Hz and 240 bpm (4 x 60 = 240) and so on.

This simple sum (Hz x 60 = bpm) can be used to calculate the harmonic bpm for any Hz frequency. Remember that if the resulting bpm is too high, you can just divide it by 2 a few times to get lower octaves that will still be in perfect harmony. You can actually use any octave of 60 (7.5, 15, 30) and it will still work, you will just get a lower octave of the same bpm.

Converting Hz to bpm

Hz	X 60 =	Bpm
1	X 60 =	60
2	X 60 =	120
4	X 60 =	240
8	X 60 =	480
16	X 60 =	960
32	X 60 =	1920
64	X 60 =	3840
128	X 60 =	7680
256	X 60 =	15360

What is amazing about this is that if you play a drumbeat at 15360 bpm it will not sound like a beat. It will play an exact 256 Hz audio tone with its timbre defined by the type of drum sound that you used. Now you can see that all frequencies on both sides of the chart above are really octaves of each other, and are all actually playing the same note.

You can also start with a bpm and then work out the harmonic Hz frequencies by reversing the sum (120 bpm divided by 60 equals 2 Hz). Then just raise 2 Hz by a few octaves to get a nice frequency for the bassline / root pitch of your song. You can also use other octaves of 60 for this calculation to get a higher octave (for example 120 bpm / 15 = 8 Hz).

Converting bpm to Hz

Bpm	/ 60 =	Hz
60	/ 60 =	1
120	/ 60 =	2
240	/ 60 =	4
480	/ 60 =	8
960	/ 60 =	16
1920	/ 60 =	32
3840	/ 60 =	64
7680	/ 60 =	128
1536	/ 60 =	256

This obviously works with any number. Just divide any bpm or multiply any Hz frequency by an octave of 60, and adjust them by octaves to get the range that you want. When using this method to make your music, you will find that it will be in very good harmony with itself. Your drumbeats and tempo synced effects will be in harmony with your audio, and if you use the lower octaves as Hz based binaural beats, they will be in harmony with all aspects as well. Also, any tempo synched effects or audio "glitches" with quantize settings above 1/32 will generate "tones" that are perfectly in tune with your music. Straight quantize settings will give you octaves of your base frequency, while triplet settings will give you octaves of its perfect fifth.

If you take a close look at some audio clips of the lower octaves of C = 256 Hz (in a DAW music project) with your tempo set to the correct harmonic bpm of 120 bpm, you will see that the number of waves in each note's waveform now fits exactly into your grid quantize (see following image).

In this image:

Orange = 120 bpm typical trance kick/bass with harmonic audio frequency of C = 32 Hz on the bass synth.

Yellow = plain 8hz, 16hz and 32 Hz saw tooth waves (octaves of C) for comparison.

Now you can easily see how they all line up in perfect harmony / geometry. I used trance as an example because of the clear beats, but this works for all music.

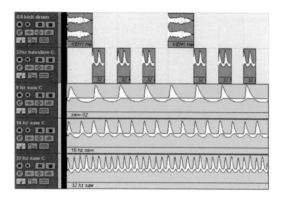

When working like this you can do some amazing things, like cutting just one peak of a waveform and repeating it to make a new and still perfectly tuned one. Then you can adjust the volume of each slice instead of using normal envelope settings, or go right into it and process the slices individually making the sound do crazy things. I can't list everything here because the possibilities opened by aligning everything like this seem to be endless.

As you can imagine, this geometry is mirrored inside your head when you listen to this music, making for some well aligned brain waves. I did some research and it turns out that I am not the only one who thought of this, either. In modern times people have discovered that classical music, especially Baroque music played at around 60 / 120 bpm and based around the C major scale, will have what they call the "Mozart effect". This is said to have many benefits such as enhanced creativity, more focused thoughts, balanced brainwaves etc. The harmonic bpm for C in 440 Hz based equal temperament is actually 122.636 bpm, but orchestras are not digital and can't actually play at exactly 120 bpm, so this is all close enough.

The next chart has all the harmonic Hz octaves for 120 bpm, some typical sound examples, and the brainwave states they generate. Because each brainwave state covers one octave the quantize ratios, sound examples, and brainwave states are correct for any other bpm between 120 and 240. Obviously with other bpms the Hz will be different and the note will not be C.

Hz	Sound examples	Brainwave state
1 Hz	1/2 = Half time snr-drum	Low delta
2 Hz	1/4 = Straight trance kick	Delta
4 Hz	1/8 = Double time hi-hat	Theta
8 Hz	1/16 = Kbbb kick-bass	Alpha
16 Hz	1/32 = Drum roll	Beta
32 Hz	1/64 = Very low C bass	Gamma
64 Hz	1/128 = C bass	High gamma
128 Hz	C mid bass	
256 Hz	Middle C	
512 Hz	C	
1024 Hz	C	
2048 Hz	C	
4096 Hz	C	
8192 Hz	C	
16384 Hz	Human hearing range ends	

It is worth noting that each brainwave state also has different levels. For example, with a song at 120 bpm with octave matched 1 Hz low delta, 2 Hz delta and 4 Hz theta brainwaves will make you quite calm. With the same song at 180 bpm with its octave matched 1.5 Hz low delta, 3 Hz delta and 6 Hz theta brainwaves will make you feel quite active, even though the waves all fall into the same states. This means that your choice of bpm is a very important factor. If you want some ideas about the properties of various bpms, the later chapter on chakras has some good charts that should help. Generally, however, what different people consider to be fast or slow varies a lot, so this is often best left to personal taste.

If you want to use software to generate brainwaves that are in time with your bpm, you may need to enter both numbers (Hz and bpm) into your software. For this to work both numbers must have no more than 2 or 3 decimals. This is because all software has a decimal limit, and in most music software this is no more than 2 or 3 digits (2.62565, for example, has too many while 2.25 is not so bad, and 2 is very good). Because your brainwave frequency also needs a higher octave to use as a reference pitch for your scale, these Hz frequencies need to be rather special numbers. Only certain bpms will have such numbers as Hz frequencies, and only certain Hz frequencies will have them as bpms.

The following chart is useful if you need a bpm and a matching low Hz brainwave frequency with a low decimal count. It covers one octave, so the Hz frequencies cover one brainwave state which is delta in this case. Just multiply or divide the numbers by 2 a few times for the other brainwave states, reference pitches for basslines, or slower bpms. The Hz frequencies are special and can be multiplied by 2 forever without growing another decimal. Some of the Hz frequencies can be divided by 2 many times for lower brainwaves, while some of them will grow decimals quite quickly. This is just a basic list of fairly useful numbers; there are more refined ones later in this book.

Low decimal Hz / bpm combinations	
120 bpm = 2.0 Hz	180 bpm = 3.0 Hz
126 bpm = 2.1 Hz	186 bpm = 3.1 Hz
132 bpm = 2.2 Hz	192 bpm = 3.2 Hz
138 bpm = 2.3 Hz	198 bpm = 3.3 Hz
144 bpm = 2.4 Hz	204 bpm = 3.4 Hz
150 bpm = 2.5 Hz	210 bpm = 3.5 Hz
156 bpm = 2.6 Hz	216 bpm = 3.6 Hz
162 bpm = 2.7 Hz	222 bpm = 3.7 Hz
168 bpm = 2.8 Hz	228 bpm = 3.8 Hz
174 bpm = 2.9 Hz	234 bpm = 3.9 Hz

There is an old numerology trick where you add all of the digits in a number together until you get a single digit. If you do it to these bpms, a repeating pattern of 3-9-6-3-9-6-3-9-6 emerges: 1+2+0=3 - 1+2+6=9 and so on. Nikola Tesla said, "If only you knew the magnificence of 3, 6 and 9, then you would have the key to the universe." So, it is interesting to find this pattern hiding in this collection of mathematically useful numbers.

If you are using standard equal temperament tuning, it is easy to adjust your bass frequency to match your bpm using master tune and Hz checking / guitar tuning software or hardware. If your synth has no master tune setting, you can choose a bpm in the following chart and make your track in the key on the far left of that row. These bpms are for each note in normal 440 Hz equal temperament with no master tune adjustments. You can trim the long bpm's to suit your DAW, and it will still be quite accurate sonically (just use 122.636 bpm / 129.929 bpm etc.)

440 Hz equal temp harmonic bpm's			
	Hz	BPM (low octave)	BPM (high octave)
C	261.625565	61.318491796875	122.63698359375
C#	277.182631	64.964679140625	129.92935828125
D	293.664768	68.82768	137.65536
D#	311.126984	72.920386875	145.84077375
E	329.627557	77.256458671875	154.51291734375
F	349.228231	81.850366640625	163.70073328125
F#	369.994423	86.717442890625	173.43488578125
G	391.995436	91.8739303125	183.747860625
G#	415.304698	97.33703859375	194.6740771875
A	440.000000	103.125	206.25
A#	466.163762	109.25713171875	218.5142634375
B	493.883301	115.753898671875	231.50779734375
C	523.251131	122.636983828125	245.27396765625

If you choose your bpm first and find that you don't like the sound of the bass that goes with it, using an octave of the fifth of the actual frequency also works very well because then your triplet quantize settings will be octaves of your bass frequency. Remember that with equal temperament the fifth is slightly "out of tune" and is not exactly the same as the perfect triplets in your quantize settings, which are the same as the perfect fifth in the harmonic series (and in the Pythagorean and Ptolemy scales in the next chapters). The equal temperament fifth is not that different to the harmonic fifth though, so it does still work quite well for this.

The Pythagorean scale

Up until now we have been working mainly with octaves and some harmonics. Now we will explore different musical scales. To work with these scales I use free software called "Scala". With this software you can make any of the scales in this book into tuning files that can be loaded into various software and hardware synthesizers. But you will find out exactly how to make and use these files in the later chapter on tuning instruments. So, for now, when I talk about setting scales to different reference pitches, or when I show charts of frequencies from scales, just keep in mind that in a later chapter I will show you how to make and use these scales with various synthesizers.

As you know, most pleasant musical sounds are made from sine waves arranged according to the harmonic series. So, finding a scale that is in tune with this will help to reduce internal disharmony in your music by aligning the melodies with the harmonic intervals in the sounds used to play them. Obviously you could just use the harmonic series as a music scale, but with our 12 key keyboards this can be tricky. For this reason, it is often better to use it as a source and extract useful bits from it instead.

The equal temperament scale is not so great for exact Hz work. The default reference pitch around which the equal temp scale is built is A = 440 Hz. So, all the A's are octaves of 440 Hz and the rest of the notes are equally spaced around this frequency (exactly 100 "cents" between each note, to be precise). When you try to use this scale with brainwaves or harmonic bpm you will find that all of the other notes, including the fifth, have "irrational numbers" as Hz frequencies. These never end and go on to infinity e.g. 281.625643676...Hz. These numbers are not much good for finding lower octaves for use as brainwaves or harmonic bpms, because it is impossible to type them into any software.

The software (Scala) that I use to work with scales (and used to calculate this chart) cannot show more than 6 decimals. So, the numbers are longer than what you see here. Because most music software only allows 2 or 3 decimals, to be sure that a number is usable it is best if it has a zero at the end like 440.000 does. If not, you must be very sure that there is not another hidden number at the end that the software won't show you (e.g. 391.995436???).

Equal temperament:

C	261.625565 Hz
C#	277.182631 Hz
D	293.664768 Hz
D#	311.126984 Hz
E	329.627557 Hz
F	349.228231 Hz
F#	369.994423 Hz
G	391.995436 Hz
G#	415.304698 Hz
A	440.000000 Hz
A#	466.163762 Hz
B	493.883301 Hz

The A = 440 Hz based equal temperament scale only has one "nice" frequency and that is 440Hz itself. So, you could make music in A at its harmonic, 103.1250 bpm, but that is very limiting for making many different songs. It also has irrational intervals between its notes which don't mirror the harmonic series exactly, and so are not in perfect vibrational harmony with each other. The only real harmonic interval in this scale is the octave which is the same as the octave in the harmonic series, otherwise the rest are just close estimates.

What you need to look at is the spacing between the notes in your scale. It would be nice, for example, if the fifths in your scale could be perfect harmonic fifths, then your triplet quantize settings will match them perfectly. Fortunately there is a scale that not only contains a perfect fifth, but is actually constructed entirely out of them and their octaves. It is called the Pythagorean scale.

This scale is nice because it is not too different from the normal equal temperament scale. Our modern day equal temperament scale was most likely based on the Pythagorean or a similar scale, so it is not really that strange that they sound quite similar. The main musical difference between them is that an equal temperament scale with its evenly spaced notes will sound the same in any key, while the Pythagorean scale sounds more harmonious than equal temperament in some keys but more out of tune in others. The one thing that is not so good about the Pythagorean scale is its major thirds. They are quite odd-sounding and could even be called "out of tune". I have devised a way of fixing most of these, but I will get to that after explaining how the original scale works.

It is said that the idea of using perfect fifths and their octaves to make scales was first thought of by Pythagoras. He was born around 570 BC on the island of Samos. Because he lived so long ago, however, details of his life are hard to come by. To make matters worse, he did not write his ideas down. So, what we do know about him was written hundreds of years after he died. He is said to have traveled to various places, including Egypt and Babylon, where he studied in various mystery schools before setting up his own sect in Croton, Greece. It was these "Pythagoreans" who much later, after the death of Pythagoras himself, influenced Socrates and his students, Aristotle and Plato, to follow a similar path. This is important to us because these people formed the basis for much of western civilization as we know it today.

Pythagoras had many very interesting ideas. For example, he believed that higher vibrational beings of extreme intelligence existed on other higher vibrational planets, with the highest ones being non-physical, almost like light. He also believed in reincarnation and thought that you should not become too attached to Earthly things, so that you could break this cycle and move up to a higher reality in your next life. He also believed that all the planets emitted sounds as they moved through space, and that these sounds made a perfect harmonic chord almost like a giant monochord. He called this sound "the music of the spheres". One of his most famous sayings was "All things are number", which makes a lot of sense if you study his work.

Stack of fifths

So how did Pythagoras make this scale using only octaves and perfect fifths? Well, there is no proof that he ever actually made the full 12 tone scale. History says that he only really used octaves and fifths to make tetrachords, which are sets of 4 notes, and that it was actually medieval musicians who used his theory to develop the first 12 tone scales. To do this they must have started by repeating a perfect fifth 11 times to make a stack of fifths.

Such a stack contains all 12 notes in the standard Pythagorean scale (that Pythagoras never actually made). There is an obvious problem, though; the gaps between the notes are far too big to be a very good scale for music. In response, they must have used the law of octaves, bringing each note down by one or more octaves to make a nice 12 tone scale that fitted into one octave, and so could be repeated over many octaves, making the full piano scale.

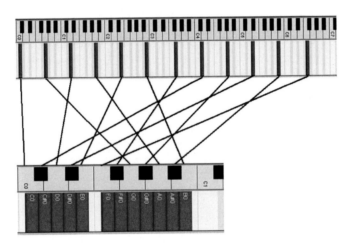

Although the stack of fifths starts with C, the first 7 notes in it make up a G major scale which also covers a full octave (when adjusted into one octave). The first medieval scales did have 7 keys with the others being added later, so it is quite probable that the first Pythagorean scale actually had 7 keys. I don't really know all of the history, though, and am more interested in dissecting the scale itself.

The next image shows the same thing as the previous image but with Hz frequencies. The green highlighted blocks show the notes shifted into one octave as in the previous image.

The horizontal columns show these frequencies over octaves, so when you move one row downward the frequency gets multiplied by 2, and when you move one row upward it gets divided by 2.

If you move one block to the right the frequency gets multiplied by 3, and if you move one block to the left it gets divided by 3 (perfect fifth + 1 octave). This octave does not matter because you can just move one block upwards in the chart, lowering it by an octave to find the actual fifth.

Stack of fifths with octaves											
C	G	D	A	E	B	F#	C#	G#	D#	A#	F
											345.9902
										320.6601	691.9804
										461.3203	1383.9609
									307.5468	922.6406	2767.9218
									615.0937	1845.2812	5535.8437
								410.0625	1230.1875	3690.5625	11071.687
							273.375	820.125	2460.375	7381.125	22143.375
							546.75	1640.2	4920.75	14762.25	44286.75
						364.5	1093.5	3280.5	9841.5	29524.5	88573.5
1	3	9	27	81	243	729	2187	6561	19683	59049	177147

C	G	D	A	E	B	F#	C#	G#	D#	A#	F
2	6	18	54	162							
4	12	36	108	324							
8	24	72	216								
16	48	144	432								
32	96	288									
64	192										
128	384										
256											

A person can use this method to find the perfect fifth of any frequency in the chart, just move one block to the right and one block upwards. In this way we can see that the fifth of 256 Hz is 384 Hz, and for 288 Hz it is 432 Hz and so on.

There is a better way to express this, and that is by using ratios. The ratio for the perfect fifth, for example, is written as 3/2. This means that you can multiply any frequency by 3 and then divide it by 2 to find its perfect fifth as a new frequency.

Perfect fifth 3/2				
D				A
288	X 3 =	864	/ 2 =	432

All 12 notes in the Pythagorean scale actually have their own ratios, and they all work in the same way as the 3/2 ratio described above. Just multiply your "perfect prime" by the first number in the ratio and divide it by the second.

Here is a chart showing one octave of the Pythagorean scale and all its ratios with A as the reference pitch (the ratios tell you the relationship that each note has to A). These are the standard ratios from the Pythagorean scale in the "software Scala" (I did not calculate them from the stack of fifths chart above). For some reason, setting C = 256 Hz as your starting frequency (unison, perfect prime) using these ratios does not give you all the same frequencies as in the above stack of fifths chart. Using A = 432 Hz, however, does. I don't know why this is so, but I do wonder if it has something to do with A being our reference pitch today and not C.

Pythagorean Scale			
A	1/1	Unison, perfect prime	216.0000 Hz
A#	2187/2048	Apotome	230.6601 Hz
B	9/8	Major whole tone	243.0000 Hz
C	32/27	Pythagorean minor third	256.0000 Hz
C#	81/64	Pythagorean major third	273.3750 Hz
D	4/3	Perfect fourth	288.0000 Hz
D#	729/512	Pythagorean tritone	307.5468 Hz
E	3/2	Perfect fifth	324.0000 Hz
F	6561/4096	Pythagorean augmented fifth	345.9902 Hz
F#	27/16	Pythagorean major sixth	364.5000 Hz
G	16/9	Pythagorean minor seventh	384.0000 Hz
G#	243/128	Pythagorean major seventh	410.0625 Hz
A	2/1	Octave	432.0000 Hz

There is one fact about ratios which I will explain fully later; this is that ratios with smaller numbers generally sound better than ones with larger numbers. In this scale, the notes with larger ratios came from the right side of the stack of fifths, while the ones with smaller ratios came from the left side. These ratios are telling you each note's relationship to A, which is near to the left of the stack of fifths. When you play this scale in A, you will hear that notes which came from the left of the stack really do sound great together, while that ones that came from the right, like G#, D#, A# and F, don't fit with them so well.

If you look at the Hz frequencies in the full stack of fifth chart earlier in this chapter, you will see that they also have more decimals as you go higher / further to the right side of the chart. The same thing happens if you want to use harmonic bpms. The lowest numbers are good for entering into the bpm settings in your music software, with their limited decimal capacity. As you can see, however, the bpms also get messier with more decimals as you go higher up the stack of fifths. I ended the following chart on B, because the bpms higher than that only get larger.

C	G	D	A	E	B
1	3	9	27	81	243
2	6	18	54	162	
4	12	36	108	324	
8	24	72	216		
16	48	144	432		
32	96	288			
64	192				
128	384				
256					
Bpm	Bpm	Bpm	Bpm	Bpm	Bpm
120	180	135	101.25	151.875	227.8125

This is a very good example the how patterns in numbers can tell you all about vibrations, without you even needing to hear them as sounds. In this situation the cause of the problems, which looking at these numbers makes easy to see and playing the scale makes easy to hear, is actually a known and much studied thing called the "Pythagorean error".

Before I explain this error and my way of "fixing" it, I must point out that the Pythagorean scale is not all that bad. The first 4 notes do have fairly small numbers, so it is good for harmonic bpm / brainwave work if played in C, G, D or A. Because all of the fifths in this scale are perfect, they will also match your triplet quantize settings perfectly no matter what key you play in. So if, for example, your song is in C = 256 Hz at 120 bpm, then the "tones" that high triplet quantize settings generate will be octaves of G = 384 Hz.

The Pythagorean error

If you look at a stack 12 fifths and one of 7 octaves on a normal synthesizer, you will find that a stack of 7 octaves and 12 fifths eventually end up on the same note again, that high C on the far right of the two images below.

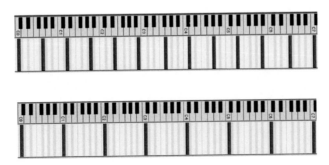

Well this is not the case with perfect fifths and octaves, a stack of 7 octaves (2/1) and a stack of 12 pure fifths (3/2) never quite meet up at all. This is because the stack of 12 perfect fifths is actually slightly longer than a stack of 7 octaves, which makes the twelfth C in a stack of perfect fifths slightly higher than the seventh octave of the first C in the same stack. In the actual scale we use an octave of the first C and not this slightly high C, but this means that the frequencies just below it in the stack are not in good harmony with it. There are people who use stretched octaves that are slightly wider than 2/1 to lesson this drift, but I have not had much luck with that using software.

In the next chart I have extended the Pythagorean stack of fifths + octaves by one more step after the top F, and lowered it by octaves to reach the same C as the first one again. Now you can see that while C is 512 Hz in the bottom left corner, the C in the top right corner is 518.9853 Hz.

Stack of pure fifths + last C												
C	G	D	A	E	B	F#	C#	G#	D#	A#	F	C
												518.9853
												1037.9707
												2075.9414
												4151.8828
												8303.7656
												16607.531
												33215.062
												66430.125
												132860.25
												265720.5
1	3	9	27	81	243	729	2187	6561	19683	59049	177147	531441

2												
4													
8													
16													
32													
64													
128													
256													
512													

This drift creates those large ratios, messy numbers, and disharmony between notes that are far from each other in the stack. In the final reduced scale these bad notes are called "wolves". With the exception of F, the really bad wolves are all black keys. So, you can use only the white ones and the black key F# to make a nice 7 tone G major scale. It will sound okay if you only use these 7 notes because they are the first 7 notes from the stack of fifths, and so they all have fairly small ratios in relation to A. This is easy to see in the stack of fifths where A is right in the center with C-G-D to the left and E-B-F# to the right of it. I have always found that A minor is a very good key for this scale, now I can see why it works so well. When using only these 7 notes you will actually be making "modal music" which is really a secret sauce for making hit songs, but I will get into that later.

I have found a way to adjust all 12 notes so they fit together much better. I call this the "Pythagorean Zodiac scale" or simply the "Pythagorean F# = 720 Hz variation". When I want to make music that changes keys a lot this is my scale of choice. If you want to try it, look for its tuning files under "files" in my Facebook group "Life, the Universe and 432 Hz".

To make this scale I chopped the stack of fifths in half right in the middle between B and F#. Then I made the fifth between them smaller, dragging the right half of the stack lower until the top C was as close to 512 Hz as I could get it without using a "messy" number for my new F#. I found that lowering F#, which was 729 Hz, to 720 Hz brought the top C down to 524880 Hz, which had 512.578125 as a lower octave and was very close to 512 Hz. Because these two C's are so close, this adjustment makes the notes right at the top of the stack like D#, A# and F sound much better with 512 Hz and the rest of the scale than before. Because the fifth between B and F# is so flat, this scale does not sound so good in B. This does not bother me, though, as playing B and F# together hurts my hand, so I don't often do it anyway.

Split stack of pure fifths (Pythagorean Zodiac / F# = 720 Hz variation)												
C	G	D	A	E	B	F#	C#	G#	D#	A#	F	C
												512.578125
												1025.15625
												2050.3125
												4100.625
												8201.25
												16402.5
												32805
												65610
												131220
												262440
1	3	9	27	81	243	720	2160	6480	19440	58320	174960	524880

2												
4												
8												
16												
32												
64												
128												
256												
512												

The new F# = 720 Hz, C# = 2160 Hz and G# = 6480 Hz all have a nice small 5/4 major third relationship with higher octaves of D = 9 Hz, A = 27 and E = 81 Hz respectively. So, D to F#, A to C# and E to G# in any octave will have this 5/4 major third. This makes the scale sound much better in these keys, as the original Pythagorean scale had very large ratios in its major thirds.

The best way to play this scale is to use one of the white keys: C, D, E, F, G or A (but not B) as the root key for your song. Then you will have many good sounding options for major and minor chords that include some of the black keys.

I have not calculated all of the ratios in this scale, but it is obvious that improvements have been made. If you look at the Hz frequencies in both scales when the notes are shifted into one octave, you can see that all of the numbers now end with a zero. So, adjusting the stack of fifths in this way has simplified its Hz frequencies.

| | Pythagorean scales | |
	Standard	Zodiac variation
C	256.000000 Hz	256.000000 Hz
C#	273.375000 Hz	270.000000 HZ
D	288.000000 Hz	288.000000 Hz
D#	307.546875 Hz	303.750000 Hz
E	324.000000 Hz	324.000000 Hz
F	345.990234 Hz	341.718750 Hz
F#	364.500000 Hz	360.000000 Hz
G	384.000000 Hz	384.000000 Hz
G#	410.062500 Hz	405.000000 Hz
A	432.000000 Hz	432.000000 Hz
A#	461.320313 Hz	455.625000 Hz
B	486.000000 Hz	486.000000 Hz
C	512.000000 Hz	512.000000 Hz

Some of these numbers actually have an interesting history. F# = 720 Hz with its lower octaves of 360, 180, 90 and 45, for example, have been used to divide the circle for thousands of years. C# = 270 Hz is also special as it has a higher octave of 2160 Hz, which is the amount of years that the Earth takes to pass through one zodiacal age (hence my naming of this scale). 256, 384, 288 and 432 have been also used to simplify calculations for thousands of years, so it's nice to have all of these numbers in one scale.

Here are the harmonic bpms for this scale. C, D, E, F#, G, A and B have usable bpms. The longer ones can be trimmed but then you will lose some accuracy. This chart can also be used for the original Pythagorean scale, as the 4 notes in it that had good numbers (C, G, D and A) are the same in this version.

Note	Pythagorean Zodiac	Bpm	Bpm
C	256 Hz	60	120
C#	270 Hz	63.28125	126.5625
D	288 Hz	67.5	135
D#	303.750 Hz	71.19140625	142.3828125
E	324 Hz	75.9375	151.875
F	341.718750 Hz	80.09033203125	160.1806640625
F#	360 Hz	84.375	168.75
G	384 Hz	90	180
G#	405 Hz	94.921875	189.84375
A	432 Hz	101.25	202.5
A#	455.6250 Hz	106.787109375	213.57421875
B	486 Hz	113.90625	227.8125
C	512 Hz	120	240

Some of these Hz frequencies have nice small whole numbers in their lowest octaves and are good for brainwave work. They all show up in the Ptolemy scale in the next chapters, though, so you can see them in the brainwave charts there.

There is one thing about octaves and fifths that I just had to add at the end of this chapter: If you multiply any number by 2 to find its higher octaves, you will find octaves of the first 4 notes in a stack of fifths starting with that number in the end digits of these higher octaves. The following chart shows 27 octaves of C = 1 Hz with these fifths (G, D and A) highlighted.

1, 2, 4, 8, 16, 32, 64, 128, 256, 512 (C = 256)

10**24**, 20**48**, 40**96**, 81**92**, 163**84**, 327**68** (G = 384)

655**36**, 1310**72**, 2621**44**, 524**288**, 1048**576**, 2097152, 4194304, 8388608 (D = 288)

16777**216**, 33554**432**, 67108**864** (A = 432)

I find this interesting, as 4 fifths is about as far as you can go with a stack of fifths before the Pythagorean error takes hold.

Ratios and vibration

To understand ratios better it helps to see them from a physical / vibratory perspective. As you may remember from the chapter on brainwave entrainment, when two sounds are slightly out of tune they create a wobble known as a beat. Well, the same thing applies to notes in a scale between which you will always find monoaural beats. You can calculate the beat between any two frequencies precisely by subtracting the smaller one from the larger one. When you compare this beat frequency to the frequencies of the notes themselves, it is easy to see why intervals with small whole numbered ratios sound so good.

If, for example, you have a starting frequency of 192 Hz, its 5/4 major third will be 240 Hz. If you subtract 192 from 240 you will have 48 Hz, which is an octave of 192 Hz. As you can imagine, having a beat frequency that is an octave of the root frequency gives an interval a very stable vibration and, therefore, a very sweet sound. This works when you use any Hz frequency as the root, as long as the ratio between the two tones is 5/4 then the beat frequency will always be an octave of the root. Here are two more examples:

320 Hz to 400 Hz = a 5/4 major third and has a beat frequency of 80 Hz (80 x 4 = 320).

257.752 Hz to 322.190 Hz = a 5/4 major third and has a beat frequency of 64.438 Hz (64.438 x 4 = 257.752).

It is the same with the 3/2 perfect fifth; its beat frequency will also always be an octave of its root no matter what frequency the root is. All intervals with small whole numbered ratios don't have beats that are octaves of their root. They do all have beats that are close harmonics of it, though. In the 6/5 minor third, for example, the beat frequency x 5 = the root frequency, while for the 4/3 perfect fourth it is an octave of the fourth of the root, and not the root itself. All of these are very harmonic combinations, though, which is why these intervals sound so good.

With equal temperament and its infinitely large ratios, the beat frequencies are never perfect octaves or harmonics of the notes frequencies. This makes them quite messy as they don't vibrate so well with the notes. The images below are both of a C major third played using the same sound on the same synth. The top one is a harmonic major third with a ratio of 5/4, while the bottom one is a normal equal temperament major third with infinitely large numbers in its ratios. The lower one is messier because the mono-aural beats are not harmonics of the root frequency, so there are more random beats making the sound more unstable. This instability gets reflected in your brainwaves, making you feel more wobbly than with harmonic intervals.

Harmonic tuning vs equal temperament

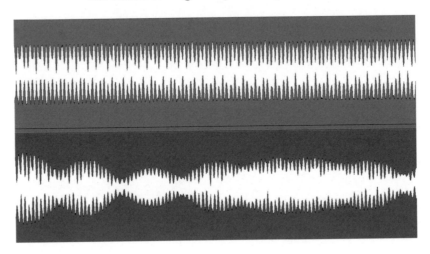

If you are a music producer you will know that stable sounds also need less compression, so it is quite true that harmonic intervals can be played louder than wobbly ones without needing as much. This applies to your whole production; if you use the correct harmonic bpm with a small ratio based scale, then everything will align even better with even less random peaks.

For an interval to sound good and to have harmonic beats, the higher tone needs to vibrate perfectly over the lower one. In the image of the harmonic series below, you can see how ratios actually vibrate. This chart only goes up to the seventh harmonic, and so you can only see ratios with numbers below 7 in them here. Now you can see how 3 waves over 2 (3/2) = perfect fifth, 4 waves over 3 (4/3) = a perfect fourth, 5 waves over 4 (5/4) = major third, 6 waves over 5 (6/5) = minor third, or any other combination of these harmonics, will fit perfectly into each other. Remember that the top wave can be any frequency. If it was 100 Hz then 2 would be 200, 3 would be 300, and so on, and they will still fit perfectly into each other.

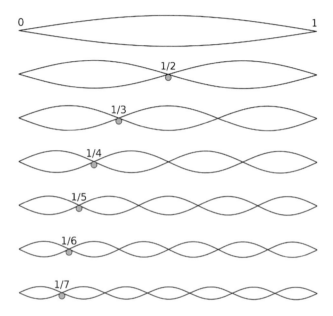

The following chart shows the names of the intervals between harmonics 1 to 7. The number above and below each interval name combine to make its ratio.

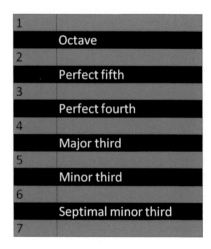

In the following chart the harmonic series has been arranged with each octave in a new row. The interval names tell you how each harmonic relates to the red "octave" at the top of that row, and these red "octave" blocks are all octaves of the fundamental (root) on the far left. While the intervals repeat over octaves, making the ratios 3/2, 6/4 and 12/8 all correct for the perfect fifth, and 5/4 or 12/8 for the major third and so on, people normally use the one closest to the root with the smallest numbers to express each interval.

1 Root	2 Octave	4 Octave	8 Octave
			9 Major whole tone
		5 Major third	10 Major third
			11 semi-augmented fourth
	3 Perfect fifth	6 Perfect fifth	12 Perfect fifth
			13 Tridecimal neutral sixth
		7 Harmonic seventh	14 Harmonic seventh
			15 Classic Major seventh

We already know that intervals with small numbered ratios sound better than ones with large numbers. Now we can see that these small numbered ratios are found closer to the fundamental in the harmonic series, while the large numbered ones are found further away from it (obviously!). When looking at it like this we can see an "order of harmoniousness" for each interval. First and most harmonious is the octave (2/1), then the perfect fifth (3/2), then the perfect fourth (4/3), major third (5/4), minor third (6/5) and so on.

When you go higher than the sixth harmonic you will find that certain harmonics are dissonant and that the order is so linear. The septimal minor third found between harmonics 6 and 7, for example, is quite dissonant when compared to the major whole tone between harmonics 8 and 9, even though it is found lower in the series (this will be explored in the next chapter). Generally however, intervals found closer to the fundamental in the harmonic series do sound better than ones found farther away from it.

If you think about the feelings that these intervals give you when played, even with equal temperament tuning, it gets quite interesting. Up to the fourth harmonic (octave / fifth / fourth) is more simple and enlightening (without emotions and thoughts). Between the fourth and sixth harmonics you have the happy and sad major and minor thirds. And above that you get smaller intervals like whole tones and semi-tones that involve more complex emotions.

This is not new information. Pythagoras and the ancient Greeks often spoke of the octave, perfect fifth and perfect fourth as the best intervals of all. This order is also useful for choosing key changes and writing melodies. If you take the time to see how many epic pieces of music have an octave, fifth, or fourth as the first key change or the first note after the root in the melody, you will be quite surprised.

Remember that most musical tones are also made of sine waves arranged according to the harmonic series, and that sounds with louder harmonics up to the sixth harmonic sound rich and warm while louder harmonics above it make a sound harsher. So, it would seem that small ratios definitely are the key to having more internal harmony in your music.

Ptolemy's 7 tone just intonation scale

Just intonation is the proper name given to scales made using small whole numbered ratios, which you now know sound good for a reason. There are many different possible just intonation scales. Making one from scratch using ratios of your own invention, however, is quite hard. It makes more sense to use what has already been discovered and to build on that. After much searching I have not found a better sounding just intonation scale than the one I am about to describe. I first found it amongst the preset scales that come with the tuning software "Scala" under the name "Ptolemy's intense diatonic". It is named after Claudius Ptolemy who was born in c 90 AD. He was a music theorist, mathematician, astronomer, geographer and astrologer, and lived in Alexandria in Egypt where many of his writings were kept in the great library of Alexandria. His work also influenced our western civilization to a large degree.

There are a few versions of this scale in the "Scala" presets, but I like this one in particular (Ptolemy's intense diatonic) because it sounds very nice when played. It is really just a standard just intonation scale, but I will refer to it as the "Ptolemy scale" since there are just too many variations of this that have no actual names. It has only got 7 notes, the 7 notes that make a major scale. When it is started in C these are all of the white keys on a piano.

(do - re - mi - fa - sol - la - ti)

There is a 12 tone version of this scale which is exactly the same, only with 5 added notes (all of the black keys when it is in C). For now, however, I will only work with the 7 tone one, explaining its significance, and will move to the 12 tone version later.

This scale sounds better than the Pythagorean scale in its reference key, but not so good in certain other keys. The best keys to change to without too many of the other notes sounding "off" follows the same order of harmoniousness mentioned earlier. So, if the reference key is C, then playing in G (fifth above the root), F (fourth above the root) or E (major third above the root) will also sound good. If you play in E you will get a very nice minor scale. This works well because a major chord is actually a major third with a minor third on top of it (together they add up to a fifth). Generally, however, you want to set your reference pitch to be the same as the root key of your song.

The reason for this is that the notes in this scale are not equally spaced as they are in equal temperament. So, if you use the 7 notes that you get from one reference pitch as 7 new reference pitches, some of the notes will drift a bit to maintain perfect harmony and will not be the same in every key. This does not happen to all of the notes, only a few of them do this.

When choirs sing they naturally use intervals with small ratios and can change to any key without any problems. This is because they hear the harmonics in the notes they are singing, and automatically use those tones for other notes in the song. So, when they change keys they just shift everything in the same way that you do when you use that note as a reference pitch for the scale. There is an adaptive tuning system / algorithm called hermode tuning that tries to replicate this. I have not used it much but it may be worth trying if you have the right software (more on this in a later chapter). I prefer using tuning files however, because I like having exact Hz values for each note for my harmonic bpm / brainwave work. I also like to make music in one key or with harmonic key changes like perfect fourths, fifths, and major thirds that work well with this scale anyway.

In the following chart you can see that the numbers in its ratios are all below 16, with only 2 intervals having numbers above 6 in theirs. Because these intervals are found so close to the fundamental of the series, it has a very sweet sound.

7 tone Ptolemy scale		
C	1/1	Unison, perfect prime
D	9/8	Major whole tone
E	5/4	Major third
F	4/3	Perfect fourth
G	3/2	Perfect fifth
A	5/3	Major sixth
B	15/8	Classic major seventh
C	2/1	Octave

If you take the two numbers in any of the above ratios and find them in the following chart, you can see exactly where each interval is found in the harmonic series.

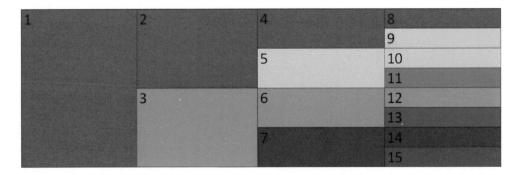

If you look at the intervals in harmonics 8 to 16, you will see that they are quite similar to those in the Ptolemy scale, but harmonics 11 and 13 have been replaced with similar but better sounding intervals found closer to the fundamental in the series, and the seventh / fourteenth harmonic has been removed.

Harmonics 8 to 16

Note	Ratio	Harmonic	Interval
C	1/1	8	Unison, perfect prime
D	9/8	9	Major whole tone
E	5/4	10	Major third
F	11/8	11	Semi-augmented fourth
G	3/2	12	Perfect fifth
A	13/8	13	Tridecimal neutral sixth
A#	7/4	14	Harmonic seventh
B	15/8	15	Classic Major seventh
C	2/1	16	Octave

Intervals with 7, 11 and 13 in their ratios have been known to sound odd since they were first discovered, so it is not strange that they have been avoided in this scale. The reason why they sound out of place is because as single tones octaves of 7, 11 and 13 don't share any harmonics with octaves of the other whole numbers from 1 to 15, while 1 to 15 (not including 7, 11 and 13) all share harmonics with each other.

To illustrate this I have made a chart using octaves of 1, 3, 5, 7, 9, 11, 13 and 15 as reference pitches for the 7 tone Ptolemy scale (this covers octaves 1, 2, 3, 4, 5, 6, 7, 8, 9, 10, 11, 12, 13, 14 and 15). I have added 27 and 45 because they often show up when you use the other numbers as reference pitches. Octaves of 1, 3, 5, 9, 15, 27 and 45 have been color-coded so that you can see which reference pitches make scales that share notes with each other. Octaves 7, 11 and 13 have not been color-coded because they don't share any notes. Apart from the 4/3 and 5/3 intervals, the rest are harmonics of lower octaves of their fundamental frequencies. So, because this scale repeats over octaves, the color-coded notes on these intervals are also showing you harmonics that are shared between octaves of 1, 3, 5 etc. when they are played as single tones.

	1	3	5	7	9	11	13	15	27	45
	C	G	E		D			B	A	F#
1/1	256.0000	384.0000	320.0000	224.0000	288.0000	352.0000	208.0000	240.0000	216.0000	360.0000
9/8	288.0000	432.0000	360.0000	252.0000	324.0000	396.0000	234.0000	270.0000	243.0000	405.0000
5/4	320.0000	480.0000	400.0000	280.0000	360.0000	440.0000	260.0000	300.0000	270.0000	450.0000
4/3	341.3333	512.0000	426.6666	298.6666	384.0000	469.3333	277.3333	320.0000	288.0000	480.0000
3/2	384.0000	576.0000	480.0000	336.0000	432.0000	528.0000	312.0000	360.0000	324.0000	540.0000
5/3	426.6666	640.0000	533.3333	373.3333	480.0000	586.6666	346.6666	400.0000	360.0000	600.0000
15/8	480.0000	720.0000	600.0000	420.0000	540.0000	660.0000	390.0000	450.0000	405.0000	675.0000
2/1	512.0000	768.0000	640.0000	448.0000	576.0000	704.0000	416.0000	480.0000	432.0000	720.0000

As you can see, octaves of 7, 11 and 13 don't share harmonics with the others or each other, which is why intervals with ratios that have 7, 11 or 13 in them sound odd when played with notes based on the other numbers.

Because octaves of 7, 11 and 13 don't share any notes / harmonics with the other numbers when they are used as reference pitches for the scale, using them will also result in songs that don't sound good on the same album / in the same DJ mix as ones with the more interconnected numbers as reference pitches.

If you are using the full harmonic bpm / brainwave system in this book, and need low decimal numbers as Hz frequencies all the way down to the lowest octaves, you will find that octaves of 1, 3, 5, 9, 15, 27 and 45 are also really good reference pitches for this. Don't get me wrong; octaves of 7, 11 and 13 do have fairly low decimal Hz frequencies when used as reference pitches for this scale, but the problem is that using them will not include octaves of 1, 2, 3, 4, 5, 6, 8, 9, 10, 12, 15, 27 and 45, whereas using octaves of 1, 3, 5, 9, 15, 27 and 45 will. Obviously these numbers are very good to have in your scale if you are trying to avoid decimals.

If you look in the previous chart you will see that the scale in G = 384 Hz is the only one that has all 7 of its notes color-coded. This means that it has 1, 3, 5, 9, 15, 27 and 45 as the lowest whole number octaves of its 7 notes and, therefore, contains 1, 2, 3, 4, 5, 6, 8, 9, 10, 12, 15, 27 and 45 and their octaves. In the following chart you can see its Hz frequencies and harmonic bpms. As you can see, they don't have too many decimals and so are good to enter into most software. These 7 numbers are what I call "magic" numbers, as their usefulness is really multifaceted.

Note	Hz	Hz	Hz	Hz	Hz	Hz	Hz	Hz	Hz	Hz	BPM	BPM
G	384	192	96	48	24	12	6	3	1.5	0.75	90	180
A	432	216	108	54	27	13.5	6.75				50.625	101.25
B	480	240	120	60	30	15	7.5	3.75			56.25	112.5
C	512	256	128	64	32	16	8	4	2	1	60	120
D	576	288	144	72	36	18	9	4.5	2.25		67.5	135
E	640	320	160	80	40	20	10	5	2.5	1.25	75	150
F#	720	360	180	90	45	22.5	11.25				84.375	168.75

In the later chapter on practical applications of brainwaves, you will see that the best plugin for adding binaural beats into music cannot accept numbers with more than 2 decimals. So, you really do want small numbers in these low octaves. If you are working with very low epsilon brainwaves between 0 and 1 Hz, you may want even smaller numbers than in the above chart. A very easy and effective way of achieving this without losing any harmony is simply to add one decimal into each of the 7 magic numbers. This will make 432 into 43.2, 384 into 38.4 and so on. Obviously adding a decimal to a number that ends in 0 is the same as just removing the 0, so numbers like 240 just become 24. Musically, adding this decimal or removing this 0 lowers the frequency by three octaves and a 5/4 major third. Because it is below and not above your starting frequency, this major third is actually called a minus major third and has a ratio of 4/5 and not 5/4.

Since the scale already has so many of these major thirds in it, adding this decimal does not mess with the overall harmony at all. Some of the notes will become frequencies that were other notes in the scale before you changed the decimal, while the others will become frequencies that were not in the scale, but that are in the 12 tone version of this scale when it has 384 Hz as its reference pitch. So, all of these frequencies are in good harmony with each other and will still sound nice on the same album or in a DJ mix. In the following image I have changed the notes' names so that you can see what they have become. Compare this chart to the previous one to see what has been changed.

Note	Hz	Hz	Hz	Hz	Hz	Hz	Hz	Hz	Hz	Hz	Hz
D#	38.4	19.2	9.6	4.8	2.4	1.2	0.6	0.3	0.15		
F	43.2	21.6	10.8	5.4	2.7	1.35					
G	48	24	12	6	3	1.5	0.75				
G#	51.2	25.6	12.8	6.4	3.2	1.6	0.8	0.4	0.2	0.1	0.05
A#	57.6	28.8	14.4	7.2	3.6	1.8	0.9	0.45			
C	64	32	16	8	4	2	1	0.5	0.25		
D	72	36	18	9	4.5	2.25					

In the following image you can see that these numbers don't get more decimals when raised by a few octaves, and so are still good as reference pitches. They also have good harmonic bpms, most of which can be found as Hz frequencies and bpms in the original 384 Hz based scale...

Note	Hz	Hz	Hz	Hz	BPM	BPM
D#	307.2	153.6	76.8	38.4	72	144
F	345.6	172.8	86.4	43.2	82	162
G	384	192	96	48	90	180
G#	409.6	204.8	102.4	51.2	96	192
A#	460.8	230.4	115.2	57.6	54	108
C	512	256	128	64	60	120
D	576	288	144	72	67.5	135

These numbers really are magical and will make almost any mathematical calculation simpler. The fact that they are also in such good musical harmony with each other makes everything work out really well for us musicians. To see all 12 of them and their low Hz + harmonic bpms in one chart, read the "Ptolemy's 12 tone just intonation scale" chapter.

To get another perspective on all of this we can look at this as a stack of fifths. In the same way that a Pythagorean scale is made from a stack of fifths, so the Ptolemy scale can also be broken down backwards into a stack of (not all perfect) fifths starting with C = 1 Hz, by simply raising or lowering the octave of each note a certain number of times. This works so well because the first 7 notes in a stack of fifths starting with C make a G major scale when adjusted into one octave.

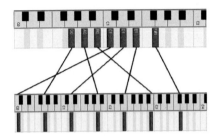

The following image contains the first seven notes from a stack of perfect fifths (Pythagorean scale) and, below it, the first seven notes from the Ptolemy stack of fifths. You can see that the first 4 frequencies in both are exactly the same, while the last three in the Ptolemy stack are slightly lower (but are still a small stack of perfect fifths). This is similar to the Pythagorean Zodiac scale, only here the fifth between A and E is smaller and E, B, and F# are slightly lower.

Ptolemy and Pythagorean scales as stacks of fifths							
				Narrow fifth			
Ptolemy stack of fifths	1	3	9	27	80	240	720
	C	G	D	A	E	B	F#
					Pure fifth		
Pythagorean stack of fifths	1	3	9	27	81	243	729
	C	G	D	A	E	B	F#

This narrow fifth is not as narrow as the one in the Pythagorean zodiac scale, so playing A and E together actually sounds alright and only wobbles a bit. When both scales are played and compared to each other, you will find that the E, B, and F# in the Ptolemy scale sound better with the other notes than E, B, and F# in the Pythagorean scale do. This is because the Ptolemy E is the pure major third of its C, with a nice small ratio of 5/4, B has the same 5/4 major third ratio with G, and F# with D, while the Pythagorean scale has no 5/4 major thirds and has much larger ratios in the same places.

If we look at the mathematical properties of these numbers we can see things from another angle. 320 Hz (Ptolemy E), for example, has the "magic" number 5 as a lower octave while 324 Hz (Pythagorean E) has the unremarkable 5.0625 Hz in the same place. The B and F# after the E also have mathematically better numbers, as B = 240 Hz is an octave of 60 Hz and F# = 720 is an octave of 360 Hz. We already know that 5, 60, and 360 (octaves of 80, 240 and 720) are great for low decimal calculations, and are closely connected to 1 in the harmonic series. The same cannot be said for 81, 243, and 729. If you lower each number by octaves to the lowest possible whole number (before decimals occur), you will see that you can't lower any of the ones of the Pythagorean stack of fifths at all. The last three notes in the Ptolemy stack of fifths, however, can be made very nice and small, revealing the magic numbers 5, 15 and 45.

Ptolemy and Pythagorean scales as stacks of fifths							
					Narrow fifth		
Ptolemy stack of fifths	1	3	9	27	80	240	720
Lowest whole number octave	1	3	9	27	5	15	45
	C	G	D	A	E	B	F#
					Pure fifth		
Pythagorean stack of fifths	1	3	9	27	81	243	729
Lowest whole number octave	1	2	9	27	81	243	729
	C	G	D	A	E	B	F#

1, 3, 9, 27, 5, 15, 45 and their octaves have been used to simplify calculations for thousands of years, and also happen to make a really good sounding music scale. So, there really does seem to be a correlation between mathematically useful numbers and musical harmony. There is a very interesting place where many of the good numbers show up together, and that is in the lists of highly composite and superior highly composite numbers.

A highly composite number is a whole number with more divisors than any smaller whole number has. The first few highly composite numbers are: 1, 2, 4, 6, 12, 24, 36, 48, 60, 120, 180, 240, 360, 720, 840, 1260… A superior highly composite number is a whole number which has more divisors than any other number scaled relative to some power of the number itself. The first few superior highly composite numbers are: 2, 6, 12, 60, 120, 360, 2520, 5040… (all superior highly composite numbers are also highly composite numbers). Some people say that the ancient Greeks knew about these numbers, as Plato himself set the ideal number of citizens in a city at 5040. The ancient Sumerians definitely knew about them, which is why they chose to divide the circle into 360 degrees, and why they decided to have 12 inches in a foot, 60 minutes in an hour, and 12 hours in a day etc.

If you are a musician and don't know what divisors and whole numbers are, a divisor is any number that can be divided by another number, while a whole number is any number with no decimals. So, 60 is great for time because it can be divided by 1, 2, 3, 4, 5, 6, 10, 12, 15, 20, 30 and 60, while 360 is very good for dividing the circle because it can be divided by 1, 2, 3, 4, 5, 6, 8, 9, 10, 12, 15, 18, 20, 24, 30, 36, 40, 45, 60, 72, 90, 120, 180 and 360. Plato's favorite 5040 is one of the best, as it can be divided by 1, 2, 3, 4, 5, 6, 7, 8, 9, 10, 12, 14, 15, 16, 18, 20, 21, 24, 28, 30, 35, 36, 40, 42, 45, 48, 56, 60, 63, 70, 72, 80, 84, 90, 105, 112, 120, 126, 140, 144, 168,

180, 210, 240, 252, 280, 315, 336, 360, 420, 504, 560, 630, 720, 840, 1008, 1260, 1680, 2520 and 5040.

If you take all of the highly composite numbers below 1000, remove any that are octaves of each other and shift them all into one octave, you will have 512, 384, 288, 240 and 360. These are all found in the Ptolemy scale when it has G = 384 Hz as its reference pitch. This shows us that highly composite numbers are a very musical set of numbers. The ones above 1000 are also harmonically connected to the ones below, they are just not found in this particular 7 tone scale.

You may have noticed that 7, 11, 13 and their octaves are not highly composite numbers; they are consecutive prime numbers, though. A prime number is a whole number greater than 1 whose only two whole-number factors are 1 and itself. Basically they are numbers that can only be divided by 1 and themselves. Obviously these are nowhere near as useful for dividing things up as highly composite numbers are.

The first few prime numbers are: 2, 3, 5, **7, 11, 13,** 17, 19, 23, 29, 31, 37, 41, 43, 47, 53, 59, 61, 67, 71, 73, 79, 83, 89, 97, 101, 103, 107, 109, 113… There are online lists that go into the 10000's, and I have not seen any recognizable magic numbers among them except for 2, 3 and 5. This is all okay, though, because 2, 3 and 5 are already so small that not dividing well does not really matter much for brainwave / scale making. The number 2 is actually also a highly composite and a superior highly composite number, so it seems like these very small numbers are quite hard to put into one box anyway.

All in all, if you ignore 2, 3 and 5 (which make a perfect inverted major chord) the rest of the prime numbers seem to be a list of non-musical / disconnected numbers that are best avoided when choosing ratios or reference pitches. In a way, you could say that they are the exact opposite of the well-organized and very harmonic highly composite / superior highly composite numbers.

Prime numbers are important, though, because all whole numbers can be written as a product of primes. In normal language, this means that you can make any whole number by multiplying prime numbers together (this is called prime factorization). What is interesting is that one of the properties of highly composite and superior highly composite numbers is that their prime factorization will always be consecutive prime numbers.

With just intonation scales, people often set a "prime limit" in the ratios. In a 5-limit scale for example the numbers in the ratios don't have prime factors higher than 5, while in a 7-limit scale they don't have prime factors higher than 7. So while prime numbers themselves are not very musical, they are still part of the deeper structures of harmony.

Light spectrum

There is an amazing thing about the 7 tone (do - re - mi - fa - sol - la – ti) major scale in G, whether it is Pythagorean, Ptolemy, or equal temperament, and that is its connection to the color light spectrum. Color is also a vibration and so colors can also be measured in Hz, although the visible light spectrum starts about 40 octaves above G = 384 Hz, so its numbers as Hz frequencies are quite large. This seems like an excellent opportunity to use the law of octaves to find audio tones that have similar properties to each color...

Light is actually measured in Angstroms with the center point for red being about 6870 Angstroms. The sum for converting Hz to Angstrom's is very complicated which is why I will just use Hz instead. So, if G = 384 Hz, then forty octaves higher would be G = 422212465065984 Hz. In the color spectrum this frequency is close to 6870 Angstroms and also sits in the band occupied by the color red.

Red is the first color on the light spectrum (the colors in a rainbow or prism), so red is the lowest vibrating color that human eyes can see. This sounds very good for a root frequency of a scale, to me; the first note in a scale around which all the rest are arranged in harmony, and so also the lowest vibrating note in the scale.

In a major scale starting with G, the highest note before the next G is F#. In the Ptolemy major scale F#'s frequency is 360 Hz. Raising 360 Hz by 40 octaves gives you 395824185999360 Hz. This frequency sits on the far right of the spectrum, in the frequency band occupied by the highest vibrating color that humans can see: violet.

So, it turns out that the light spectrum covers just under one octave, which starts about 40 octaves above G = 384 Hz. I mentioned before how sound changes properties every 8 octaves... well 8 x 5 = 40, so the light spectrum also starts at one of these eighth octave points. It is important to remember that the light spectrum is really a continuous fade from one end to the other, it is only our eyes and minds that divide it into 7 colors. But the fact that it covers just under one octave makes any scale that divides an octave into 7 parts fit over it very well, as the next note after the 7 notes (octave of the first note) will be just above the top of the spectrum. Because each color covers a band around that frequency, the 7 tones that make a G major scale in the 12 tone Pythagorean, Ptolemy, and even equal temperament scales, will all fall into the same color bands.

As usual, there are patterns to be found and things to be learned. The G major chord, for example, mirrors the three primary colors, which is quite amazing as the major chord and three primary colors are the building blocks from which more complex scales and colors (paint mixing) are made.

The next image shows the small band of visible light that we have been dealing with. I can't help but wonder if the octaves above and below (radio, microwave, infrared, ultraviolet, x-ray and gamma ray) might not follow the same patterns as visible light does. If they do mirror each other in some way, then maybe we could use our understanding of light to understand things that lie between, above and below it in the spectrum. This could even help us to understand other dimensions and higher realms, as any repeating patterns may extend further than we can see. There are 7 "levels" in the electromagnetic spectrum, so the eighth level above gamma rays must be the first level in a new set of 7 levels...

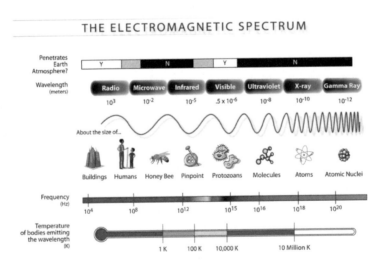

Chakra work

The color spectrum has been used in chakra work for a very long time. This is an ancient field of study, and is a good place to learn about the more esoteric side of light. When you super-impose a standard chakra chart over a G major scale, everything fits together perfectly.

7	F# = Violet	Crown	Top of head	Connection to Spirituality
6	E = Indigo	Third eye	Forehead	Intellect, wisdom
5	D = Blue	Throat	Throat	Communication, drive
4	C = Green	Heart	Chest	Love, compassion
3	B = Yellow	Solar plexus	Upper abdomen	Will power
2	A = Orange	Sacral	Lower abdomen	Sexuality, well being
1	G = Red	Root	Base of spine	Survival

Most chakra charts say that red is the lowest vibrating or "root" chakra and that violet is the highest vibrating or "crown" chakra, with the same colors for the chakras in between. So, I made a possible chakra / audio frequency chart from the 7 tone Ptolemy scale in G, matching its Hz frequencies and bpms to their matching colors 40 octaves higher.

Chakra	Note / color	Actual light frequency	Lower octave	Harmonic Bpm
Crown	F# = Violet	791648371998720 Hz	720 Hz	168.75 Bpm
Third eye	E = Indigo	703687441776640 Hz	640 Hz	150 Bpm
Throat	D = Blue	633318697598976 Hz	576 Hz	135 Bpm
Heart	C = Green	562949953421312 Hz	512 Hz	120 Bpm
Solar plexus	B = Yellow	527765581332480 Hz	480 Hz	112.5 Bpm
Sacral	A = Orange	474989023199232 Hz	432 Hz	101.25 Bpm
Root	G = Red	422212465065984 Hz	384 Hz	90 Bpm

The following chart came to me in a flash of numbers and connections. It is the same as the one above, but each color-coded horizontal row also falls into a new octave and, therefore, a different brainwave state. The vertical column marked "brainwave frequencies" covers the first 7 octaves of brainwave frequencies, and the column marked "audio frequencies" covers the next 7 octaves of audio above it. I put the octaves side by side and calculated frequencies that are octaves of each chakra frequency, and that also all falls into 14 successive octaves. Then it just about covers the full range of musical audio, all the way from the slowest beats right up to the highest tones. Basically it is just a 7 tone Ptolemy scale but with each successive note in the next octave.

I added the eighth octave to include the high gamma brainwave state and called it "spirit realm" in the chakra column. It is not a chakra, though; this octave represents the next level of reality.

Chakra	Note / color	Brainwave	Brainwave	Audio	Bpm
Spirit realm	G = Red	High Gamma	96 Hz	12288 Hz	180 Bpm
Crown	F# = Violet	Gamma	45 Hz	5760 Hz	168.75 Bpm
Third eye	E = Indigo	Beta	20 Hz	2560 Hz	150 Bpm
Throat	D = Blue	Alpha	9 Hz	1152 Hz	135 Bpm
Heart	C = Green	Theta	8 Hz	1024 Hz	120 Bpm
Solar plexus	B = Yellow	Delta	3.75 Hz	480 Hz	112.5 Bpm
Sacral	A = Orange	Low delta	1.6875 Hz	216 Hz	101.25 Bpm
Root	G = Red	Epsilon	0.75 Hz	96 Hz	90 Bpm

I think the "audio" column has a good frequency range to use for each chakra; a nice bass tone for the base chakra and a very high whistle for the crown. Remember, these are just possible frequencies, I can't say that they are exactly right. In fact, I can't even prove that chakras exist at all! If you don't believe in chakras, however, you can still make a "light spectrum" sound journey. This will still be very interesting and fitting with nature.

Remember that each color covers a band around that frequency. So, even in music tuned to A = 440 Hz with the equal temperament scale, each note in a G major scale will still fall within that color band, as will the same notes in the A = 432 Hz Pythagorean scale. I just used the Ptolemy scale here because it has nice low decimal numbers for harmonic bpm and brainwave work.

The 7 modes

If you are making a song for each chakra using any 12 tone chromatic scale, a good method is to use only the 7 notes from a G major scale to make a different 7 tone scale for each chakra. If you do this you will find that the scale for G will be a major scale.

While for E, it will be a minor one.

As you go through these 7 scales you will find that no two are the same, giving each of the 7 chakras its own unique tune or mode. The ancient Greeks, Pythagoras, Socrates and his students, Aristotle and Plato, were very interested in modes. They believed that each one mirrored an emotional state in man, and that listening to certain modes would eventually change a person so that their emotional state matched that mode. They took it a bit far by wanting to ban certain modes and instruments that could play more than one mode. At one point they actually wanted to ban all musical innovation, because they considered this freedom to be very dangerous!

The 7 modes are easy to understand when you start them in C, because then they fall on all the white notes. If you shift these modes upwards, however, starting on G to mirror the light spectrum, then you have that one black note (F#) and no F in all 7 of them. It is very interesting how some chakra charts start with G = red = base chakra, while others start with C = red = base chakra. This could be explained by the fact that red and green are complimentary colors, and are connected in a strange way. If you stare at a red object for a while and then look at a white wall you will see a green after image. If you stare at a green object you will see a red one, so it is possible to assign C to red if you think in complimentary colors. A red object actually looks red because it absorbs all colors except for red, which it reflects. So, in a way, red is not red at all, but the exact opposite. It is also worthwhile to note that C and G are a fifth apart and so are very harmonious with each other from a musical perspective.

There are actually certain sound healers that use dual systems of healing based on complimentary colors, where they first determine the "orientation" of a person and then decide whether they must use a "red" or "green" system. In this way they may use the resonant frequency of a problem or its complimentary frequency to fix it.

In the harmonic series, the fifth is the next harmonic after the octave. So, when you hear C (green) you will usually hear G (red) clearly in its harmonics, too. This is why you can make a G note on a piano ring by hitting the second C below it (the third harmonic of the C tone matches the fundamental frequency of the G tone). It is a bit off with equal temperament but it still works, showing us that sound entrainment is not only effective with octaves but also with overtones, and that it still works even if the frequency is slightly out.

The following chart shows the modes and their names as they are normally arranged, starting with the Ionian mode in C and using only the white keys. If you use complementary colors, then starting with C = red makes perfect sense and can be used in a dual healing / chakra system that uses the complementary color for each note.

B Locrian	B, C, D, E, F, G, A	Crown
A Aeolian	A, B , C, D, E, F, G	Third eye
G Mixolydian	G, A, B , C, D, E, F	Throat
F Lydian	F, G, A, B , C, D, E	Heart
E Phrygian	E, F, G, A, B , C, D	Solar plexus
D Dorian	D, E, F, G, A, B , C	Sacral
C Ionian	C, D, E, F, G, A, B	Root

If you start the modes in G instead of C, however, they mirror the actual color for each note and include F#, which is a black key, instead of F.

F# Locrian	F#, G, A, B , C, D, E	Crown
E Aeolian	E, F#, G, A, B , C, D	Third eye
D Mixolydian	D, E, F#, G, A, B , C	Throat
C Lydian	C, D, E, F#, G, A, B	Heart
B Phrygian	B, C, D, E, F#, G, A	Solar plexus
A Dorian	A, B , C, D, E, F#, G	Sacral
G Ionian	G, A, B , C, D, E, F#	Root

As you can see, you now have a mode for each of your chakras. The root chakra, for example, plays the Ionian mode which is identical to a natural major scale, while the third eye chakra plays the Aeolian mode which is identical to a natural minor scale. Although I had no idea that they had names, I discovered these modes when I was about 9-years-old. To make it easy to play piano, I noticed that if you only use all 7 white keys and left out all the black ones, then it was easy to play complicated sounding music full of key changes that always just sounded "right".

When doing this, however, I found that I could play nice chords in all of the 7 keys except for B. This is because all of the notes have their fifth among the others expect for B. To solve this I would just use F# instead of F when playing in B. Doing this essentially changed the Locrain mode, so that was no longer the same but sounded better to the ear.

B Locrian	B, C, D, E, F#, G, A, B
A Aeolian	A, B , C, D, E, F, G, A
G Mixolydian	G, A, B , C, D, E, F, G
F Lydian	F, G, A, B , C, D, E, F
E Phrygian	E, F, G, A, B , C, D, E
D Dorian	D, E, F, G, A, B , C, D
C Ionian	C, D, E, F, G, A, B , C

I am not the first person to do this. The original Gregorian scale had 8 notes so that they could have a fifth in all of the modes (their keyboards had 8 white keys and no black keys). Using the 7 white keys with F# also still fits with the color spectrum, as the actual amount of colors in the rainbow has never really been proven. Some scientists say there are only 6 while some people can see 8 or more. Since fifths fall into complimentary color bands, the colors for these 8 notes make a perfect color wheel with complimentary colors opposite each other. This does not work with only 7 colors, because then the wheel has no opposite sides.

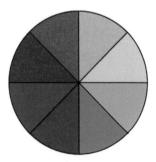

Adding this note does not change the other modes; it is only when you play the Locrian mode that you may want the option of adding it. So, you will still be following the traditional 7 modes, and can still make a chakra journey with the same 7 chakras.

When using only these notes some rules are created. If your song is in E it will have to be in E minor. If your song changes from E to C it must change from E minor to C major and so on. I would recommend trying this on a piano or synthesizer to see how well it works, and how these rules really do make good sounding music very easy to make, even for a 9-year-old.

I have met many vocalists, guitarists, and other instrumentalists who follow these same rules. This is interesting because not all instruments automatically show you the way, as a piano does with its white keys. And yet, so many great musicians still do this even though most of them don't even know why. I think this happens because even on a normal equal tempered piano these keys still closely imitate the best sounding intervals in the harmonic series, which also share the most harmonics. So, I guess, it is just natural that sensitive musicians would hear and follow this pattern.

This type of music is not new and is actually called "modal music". It was used in ancient Greece, in medieval church music and is still used today as the secret sauce in many great songs. Do yourself a favor and research this yourself. It really is used in a ridiculously large percentage of songs that have become the biggest hits in western pop culture.

Ptolemy's 12 tone just intonation scale

This scale is exactly the same as the 7 tone version, only it has 5 extra notes. It also sounds best in its reference key. Because it has 12 notes, however, you can play all 7 modes in this key. If you want to make a light spectrum or chakra journey that moves through 7 keys, the best way will be to use those 7 notes in this scale as 7 reference pitches for 7 new scales. Then you can play each of the modes in these keys while always playing the scale in its reference key. Because it sounds so good in its root key, this scale is a very good option for making house, trance or any style of music that stays in this key most of the time.

If you start it in C and use the complimentary color for each note, the 7 tone major scale falls on the white keys and mirrors the 7 main colors, while the 5 tone pentatonic scale falls on the black keys and mirrors the 5 extra hues.

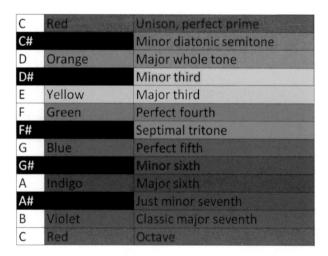

Note	Color	Interval
C	Red	Unison, perfect prime
C#		Minor diatonic semitone
D	Orange	Major whole tone
D#		Minor third
E	Yellow	Major third
F	Green	Perfect fourth
F#		Septimal tritone
G	Blue	Perfect fifth
G#		Minor sixth
A	Indigo	Major sixth
A#		Just minor seventh
B	Violet	Classic major seventh
C	Red	Octave

These 12 colors are not just random; they are really called the 12 chromatic colors. The term chromatic is derived from the Greek word "chroma" which means color. Any scale that divides an octave into 12 more or less equal parts is actually called a chromatic scale. This includes the 12 tone Pythagorean, Ptolemy and equal temperament scales.

If you arrange these 12 colors in a wheel, the complementary colors will also always be opposite each other. Color wheels like this can be very helpful if you are working on a color / sound journey and quickly need to check what color or note is complimentary to another.

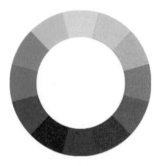

If you start the scale in G then it mirrors the actual colors and not the complementary ones, with the 5 new notes falling on the black keys and one white key F instead of the black key F#. If you look at the numbers in its ratios (following chart), you can see that they are mostly nice and small. This is a sure sign that this scale will also sound very nice, as its intervals are all found quite low down in the harmonic series. It does not contain 11 or 13 in its ratios, but it does contain 7 in the 7/5 interval between G and C#. G to C# was actually known as the devil's interval to the ancient Greeks because it sounds quite bad, so you may want to avoid it anyway... As with the 7 tone version, using G = 192 Hz / 384 Hz gives you an amazingly low decimal count in its Hz frequencies and harmonic bpms, revealing 5 new magic numbers on the notes G#, A#, C#, D# and F.

Note	Ratios	Hz frequencies over a few octaves	Bpm
G	1/1	192, 96, 48, 24, 12, 6, 3, 1.5	90 / 180
G#	16/15	102.4, 51.2, 25.6, 12.8, 6.4, 3.2, 1.6, 0.8, 0.4, 0.2, 0.1	96 / 192
A	9/8	216, 108, 54, 27, 13.5	50.625 / 101.25
A#	6/5	230.4, 115.2, 57.6, 28.8, 14.4, 7.2, 3.6, 1.8, 0.9	54 / 108
B	5/4	240, 120, 60, 30, 15, 7.5	56.25 / 112.5
C	4/3	256, 128, 64, 32, 16, 8, 4, 2, 1, 0.5	60 / 120
C#	7/5	268.8, 134.4, 67.2, 33.6, 16.8, 8.4, 4.2, 2.1	63 / 126
D	3/2	288, 144, 72, 36, 18, 9, 4.5	67.5 / 135
D#	8/5	307.2, 157.6, 76.8, 38.4, 19.2, 9.6, 4.8, 2.4, 1.2, 0.6, 0.3	72 / 144
E	5/3	320, 160, 80, 40, 20, 10, 5, 2.5	75 / 150
F	9/5	345.6, 172.8, 86.4, 43.2, 21.6, 10.8, 5.4, 2.7	81 / 162
F#	15/8	360, 180, 90, 45, 22.5	84. 375 / 168. 75

With the exception of the devil's C# they are all from the original 7 magic numbers found on the other notes, just with an added decimal. You can look at their lower octaves nearer to the middle of the chart to see this. The 5 new notes were not reached by adding this decimal, they were found by using the best sounding intervals with the smallest possible ratios. I only noticed this pattern recently, even though it was in the charts in the first edition of this book all along.

It might look as if these new Hz frequencies like 102.4 and 230.4 could be smaller, maybe just 102 and 230. But, the lower octaves of 102 and 230 have many decimals, while you can see in the previous chart that the lower octaves for 102.4 and 230.4 are very nice and small. It is the same with all 5 of them. They look funny but some of their low octaves are actually better than the low octaves of the 7 original magic numbers. This makes perfect sense when you think about that added decimal, and how 1 has become 0.1 while 9 has become 0.9 and so on.

Because adding this decimal lowers the frequency by a three octaves and 4/5 -major third, these new numbers also work very well as reference pitches for this scale, and will be in good harmony with the other 7 magic numbers. The following image has 102.4, 230.4, 268.8, 307.2 and 345.6 as reference pitches for the scale. I have color-coded the 4 original magic numbers that appear. You can actually see that 128, 288, 384 and 432 are all in the row with the 5/4 ratio. If you reverse this ratio to 4/5 and apply it to any of these 4 numbers, you will get the number at the top of its row (128 multiplied by 4 and divided by 5 = 102.4). It is interesting how these specific 4 of the 7 magic numbers appear, as they are also octaves of the first 4 numbers in the Pythagorean stack of fifths. C# does not have any of the original magic numbers connected to it, but it is connected to 384 Hz by the devil's interval, so this is understandable.

	0.1	0.9	2.1	0.3	2.7
	G#	A#	C#	D#	F
1/1	102.4000	230.4000	268.8000	307.2000	345.6000
16/15	109.2266	245.7600	286.7200	327.6800	368.6400
9/8	115.2000	259.2000	302.4000	345.6000	388.8000
6/5	122.8800	276.4800	322.5600	368.6400	414.7200
5/4	128.0000	288.0000	336.0000	384.0000	432.0000
4/3	136.5333	307.2000	358.4000	409.6000	460.8000
7/5	143.3600	322.5600	376.3200	430.0800	483.8400
3/2	153.6000	345.6000	403.2000	460.8000	518.4000
8/5	163.8400	368.6400	430.0800	491.5200	552.9600
5/3	170.6666	384.0000	448.0000	512.0000	576.0000
9/5	184.3200	414.7200	483.8400	552.9600	622.0800
15/8	192.0000	432.0000	504.0000	576.0000	648.0000
2/1	204.8000	460.8000	537.6000	614.4000	691.2000

These 5 also share many notes and harmonics with each other. I have not color-coded them but they are in the above chart.

In the following image you can see that using octaves of the other 7 magic numbers as reference pitches will sometimes include a few of these 5 new ones. Only G = 384 Hz, however, will include all of them. You can get 268.8 Hz (octave of 537.6 Hz) by using an octave of 7 as a reference pitch, showing us that it is connected to 384 Hz but via the devil's 7/5 interval and a 6/5 minor third.

	1	3	5	7	9	11	13	15	27	45
	C	G	E		D			B	A	F#
1/1	256.0000	384.0000	320.0000	224.0000	288.0000	352.0000	208.0000	240.0000	216.0000	360.0000
16/15	273.0666	409.6000	341.3333	238.9333	307.2000	375.4666	221.8666	256.0000	230.4000	384.0000
9/8	288.0000	432.0000	360.0000	252.0000	324.0000	396.0000	234.0000	270.0000	243.0000	405.0000
6/5	307.2000	460.8000	384.0000	268.8000	345.6000	422.4000	249.6000	288.0000	259.2000	432.0000
5/4	320.0000	480.0000	400.0000	280.0000	360.0000	440.0000	260.0000	300.0000	270.0000	450.0000
4/3	341.3333	512.0000	426.6666	298.6666	384.0000	469.3333	277.3333	320.0000	288.0000	480.0000
7/5	358.4000	537.6000	448.0000	313.6000	403.2000	492.8000	291.2000	336.0000	302.4000	504.0000
3/2	384.0000	576.0000	480.0000	336.0000	432.0000	528.0000	312.0000	360.0000	324.0000	540.0000
8/5	409.6000	614.4000	512.0000	358.4000	460.8000	563.2000	332.8000	384.0000	345.6000	576.0000
5/3	426.6666	640.0000	533.3333	373.3333	480.0000	586.6666	346.6666	400.0000	360.0000	600.0000
9/5	460.8000	691.2000	576.0000	403.2000	518.4000	633.6000	374.4000	432.0000	388.8000	648.0000
15/8	480.0000	720.0000	600.0000	420.0000	540.0000	660.0000	390.0000	450.0000	405.0000	675.0000
2/1	512.0000	768.0000	640.0000	448.0000	576.0000	704.0000	416.0000	480.0000	432.0000	720.0000

In the following image I have used octaves of 1, 3, 5, 7, 9, 11, 13, 15, 27 and 45 as reference pitches for the scale (remember that this covers octaves of 1, 2, 3, 4, 5, 6, 7, 8, 9, 10, 11, 12, 13, 14, 15, 27 and 45). Octaves of the original 7 magic frequencies are color-coded so that you can see shared notes / harmonics. Take note that 7, 11, and 13 don't connect at all, and that the devil's 7/5 interval does not have any magic numbers in its horizontal row. Because our eyes like the 7 harmonic divisions of an octave, color-coding the 5 new numbers with the other hues in the same chart made it very hard to see what was going on. It is fine when all 12 chromatic colors are in order, but when they are mixed up it becomes very hard to tell one shade from the next. The previous chart, however, has the exact same frequencies as this one only the 5 new numbers are color-coded, so you can just compare the two charts to get the full picture.

	1	3	5	7	9	11	13	15	27	45
	C	G	E		D			B	A	F#
1/1	256.0000	384.0000	320.0000	224.0000	288.0000	352.0000	208.0000	240.0000	216.0000	360.0000
16/15	273.0666	409.6000	341.3333	238.9333	307.2000	375.4666	221.8666	256.0000	230.4000	384.0000
9/8	288.0000	432.0000	360.0000	252.0000	324.0000	396.0000	234.0000	270.0000	243.0000	405.0000
6/5	307.2000	460.8000	384.0000	268.8000	345.6000	422.4000	249.6000	288.0000	259.2000	432.0000
5/4	320.0000	480.0000	400.0000	280.0000	360.0000	440.0000	260.0000	300.0000	270.0000	450.0000
4/3	341.3333	512.0000	426.6666	298.6666	384.0000	469.3333	277.3333	320.0000	288.0000	480.0000
7/5	358.4000	537.6000	448.0000	313.6000	403.2000	492.8000	291.2000	336.0000	302.4000	504.0000
3/2	384.0000	576.0000	480.0000	336.0000	432.0000	528.0000	312.0000	360.0000	324.0000	540.0000
8/5	409.6000	614.4000	512.0000	358.4000	460.8000	563.2000	332.8000	384.0000	345.6000	576.0000
5/3	426.6666	640.0000	533.3333	373.3333	480.0000	586.6666	346.6666	400.0000	360.0000	600.0000
9/5	460.8000	691.2000	576.0000	403.2000	518.4000	633.6000	374.4000	432.0000	388.8000	648.0000
15/8	480.0000	720.0000	600.0000	420.0000	540.0000	660.0000	390.0000	450.0000	405.0000	675.0000
2/1	512.0000	768.0000	640.0000	448.0000	576.0000	704.0000	416.0000	480.0000	432.0000	720.0000

Remember that this scale always sounds best when played in the same key as its reference pitch, or a fifth, fourth, or major third above it. So, because using G = 384 Hz as a reference pitch reveals 12 of the most mathematically useful numbers, you can use the following chart to find useful reference pitches for music in all 12 keys. If you want to see the very low octaves, there is a chart near the start of this chapter that shows them. Because they share so many notes when used as reference pitches for this scale, they will also sound very good on the same album / in the same DJ mix. Only the devil's C# may not fit so well. I have shown them in 3 different octaves so that you can see how many of the numbers are actually the same, only with an added decimal.

Note	Hz low octave	Hz mid octave	Hz high octave	Bpm
G	12	192	384	90 / 180
G#	12.8	102.4	204.8	96 / 192
A	27	216	432	50.625 / 101.25
A#	28.8	230.4	460.8	54 / 108
B	30	240	480	56.25 / 112.5
C	32	256	512	60 / 120
C#	33.6	268.8	537.6	63 / 126
D	36	288	576	67.5 / 135
D#	38.4	307.2	614.4	72 / 144
E	40	320	640	75 / 150
F	43.2	345.6	691.2	81 / 162
F#	45	360	720	84. 375 / 168. 75

If you want to try this scale, look under "files" in my FB group "Life, the universe and 432 Hz" for tuning files in these 12 keys. While it is the Ptolemy scale that led us to these 12 numbers, they are not only good as reference pitches for it. These numbers are my starting point for any kind of math based music or brainwave program making; I literally turn on my PC, open this chart and then open my DAW.

This 12 tone scale can also be deconstructed into a stack of fifths. This stack of fifths has 4 narrow fifths (marked by the horizontal lines in the next image) while the rest are all perfect fifths. It is very interesting to note once again that the Pythagorean scale with a ref pitch of A = 432 Hz and the Ptolemy scale with a ref pitch of G = 384 Hz, can both be broken down into stacks of fifths that start with C = 1 Hz, and that the narrow fifths make the other frequencies in better harmony with 1 Hz and with each other.

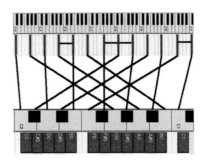

I mentioned before that if you are working with harmonic bpm you will often find that the fifth of the actual harmonic Hz frequency is more to your taste. Well, the Ptolemy scale sounds good when it is played a fifth above its reference pitch, so it will work very well for this. Because the fifth above the reference pitch is a perfect 3/2 fifth and matches the triplet quantize settings in your DAW perfectly, when you use high quantize triplet settings to get tones from tiny audio slices or fast modulation, they will be perfectly in-tune with your bassline (if it is a perfect fifth above the reference pitch). If you don't like the way the scale sounds when it is played a fifth above its reference pitch, you can just calculate the frequency of this fifth and use it as a reference pitch to make a new scale.

Astrological music

In astrology, people assign each of the 12 constellations/signs in the Zodiac to the 12 chromatic colors and the chromatic scale. Because they always start with red = Aries and follow the color spectrum upwards, using G as a reference pitch for a 12 tone chromatic scale mirrors these astrological charts very well. You could also use the complementary color system and start with C, C#, D, D#, E etc. leaving the rest of the chart the same, but I will start with G here as it is the exact octave match for red.

12 signs of the zodiac				
F#	Pisces	Fish	Neptune	Water
F	Aquarius	Water bearer	Uranus	Air
E	Capricorn	Goat	Saturn	Earth
D#	Sagittarius	Archer	Jupiter	Fire
D	Scorpio	Scorpion	Pluto	Water
C#	Libra	Scales	Venus	Air
C	Virgo	Virgin	Mercury	Earth
B	Leo	Lion	Sun	Fire
A#	Cancer	Crab	Moon	Water
A	Gemini	Twins	Mercury	Air
G#	Taurus	Bull	Venus	Earth
G	Aries	Ram	Mars	Fire

The theory behind this is that good sounding combinations of notes are meant to represent good star sign matches for people. The musical interval from one fire sign to the next, for example, is a major third while matches of these signs are known to work well among people. The same applies to the gaps between any neighboring matching signs, water to the next water, air to the next air etc. So, these signs should go very well together: Aries to Leo, Taurus to Virgo, Gemini to Libra and so on. To work out more harmonic connections you can just play on a piano to see which pairs, trio's or even more notes, sound good together to find harmonic astrological connections. At the moment of your birth there will be certain planets lined up to various signs and their constellations. According to astrologers this also influences your life. These alignments can also be expressed musically using the chart above.

Because the major chord is found so close to the fundamental in the harmonic series, it is the most harmonious 3 tone chord of all. So, this would be the chord to look out for when making connections with 3 points. For example, two fire signs that are next to each other will make a major third, and then to complete the chord all you need is the fifth. To locate that you go to the sign below the next fire sign above. For example, G (fire) to B (fire) and then D (water, which is just below the next fire). The major chord in G consists of the notes G, B, D. So, a major chord starting on Aries would be Aries, Leo and Scorpio, and for Gemini it would be Gemini, Libra and Capricorn.

You could also add an extra note / sign to make a 4 tone major 7th chord if you want to. This interval, however, is very jazzy and different so you can expect the same from people who are separated from you by this interval.

This is of great interest to me because there people called "indigo people" who are said to have indigo colored auras and a wide open third eye. They are said to be very creative, intelligent, able to see the real truth, and therefore are not good at fitting into mundane society. So, it is amazing that the seventh harmonic / major seventh is connected to the color indigo in the light spectrum and the third eye in the chakra system.

All of this very accurately describes the behavior of 7 in vibration as it represents the harmonic major seventh, which is nice as part of a harmonic major seventh chord but is quite hard to fit into most songs or use as an interval on its own. Mathematically, the number 7 also behaves differently when used as a reference pitch for the Ptolemy scale, revealing numbers that are not found in the normal "magic number grid".

As I have said I am no astrologer, this is just how I break it down using the laws of vibration. I have, however, sent this chapter to a professional astrologer and she said it is all correct according to her views on the subject.

Harmonic scales

If you want to mirror the harmonic series more directly in a scale, you may want to use its intervals in their original order and not re-arranged using ratios. This is already a done thing. A scale made by taking an octave portion of the harmonic series and repeating it over octaves is simply called a "harmonic scale". These scales seldom have 7 or 12 tones and can be hard to get used to playing on a normal keyboard. They also don't avoid odd sounding ratios and so often have a very exotic sound if you use all of their notes. In the scale making software "Scala", however, you can generate harmonic scales with simple settings for the "first" and "last" harmonic, and insert or remove notes (chapter on how to use Scala later in this book).

Harmonic scales 1 to 15

I have listened to all of the harmonic scales based on the numbers 1 to 16. As expected, the ones based on magic numbers like 1, 3, 5, 9 etc. sound the best, while the ones based on 7, 11 and 13 don't sound very good at all.

Harmonics 2 to 4, 4 to 8, 8 to 16 or 16 to 32, for example, make very nice scales because they have 1 as the lowest octave of their roots. Obviously 2 to 4 and 4 to 8 have too few notes to really be scales, but since each octave contains the ones below, you will have them in harmonics 16 to 32 anyway. You can actually find all of the scales in this chapter in harmonics 16 to 32, but I will dissect each one so you can see the intervals you get when you change the root to other harmonics.

1	2	4	8		16 Octave
					17 17th harmonic
			9		18 Major whole tone
					19 19th harmonic
		5	10		20 Major third
					21 Narrow fourth
			11		22 Undecimal semi-augmented fourth
					23 23rd harmonic
3	6	12			24 Perfect fifth
					25 Classic augmented fifth
			13		26 Tridecimal neutral sixth
					27 Pythagorean major sixth
	7	14			28 Harmonic seventh
					29 29th harmonic
		15			30 Classic major seventh
					31 31st harmonic

If you use harmonics 16 to 32 and remove the fourth, fifth, sixth and seventh that have 7, 11, 13 and 25 as lower octaves, then you will get a 12 tone scale that sounds really nice. There is more than one fourth, fifth, sixth and seventh in the full scale, so removing one of each makes good sense anyway.

Harmonics 3 to 6, 6 to 12, and 12 to 24 also sound very nice because they have 3 as a lower octave of their root. There are some odd intervals, but generally this scale is very nice to play.

1	2	4	8	16+
1	2	4	8	16 Perfect fourth
				17 2nd septendecimal tritone
			9	18 Perfect fifth
				19 Undevicesimal minor sixth
		5	10	20 Major sixth
				21 Harmonic seventh
			11	22 Undecimal neutral seventh
				23 Vicesimotertial major seventh
	3	6	12 Root	24 Octave
				25
			13 Tridecimal 2/3-tone	26
				27
		7	14 Septimal minor third	28
				29
			15 Major third	30
				31

Harmonics 5 to 10 and 10 to 20 are also very good because they have 5 as a lower octave of their root. Harmonics 10 to 20 contains a harmonic minor scale with a ratio of 6/5 in its minor third (the same minor third found in the Ptolemy scale). It also has a perfect fifth, so this is a very good option for music in a minor key if you pick the right notes.

1	2	4	8	16+
1	2	4	8	16 Minor sixth
				17 Diminished seventh
			9	18 Just minor seventh
				19 Undevicesimal major seventh
		5	10 Root	20 Octave
				21
			11 Ptolemy's second	22
				23
	3	6	12 Minor third	24
				25
			13 Semi-diminished fourth	26
				27
		7	14 Septimal tritone	28
				29
			15 Perfect fifth	30
				31

Harmonics 7 to 14, on the other hand, sound quite strange. To get a better perspective on this I will show its ratios instead of its harmonic numbers. If you look at the ratios in this scale you will see that they all have the number 7 in them, and that 3 of the intervals have the word "septimal" in them. In mathematics the word septimal actually means "relating to the number seven", explaining why these odd sounding intervals have it in their names. Because this scale has no "normal" fifths, fourths, thirds etc. it is very hard to play in a way that actually sounds good.

Harmonics 7 to 14:

1/1: root
8/7: septimal whole tone
9/7: septimal major third, BP third
10/7: euler's tritone
11/7: undecimal augmented fifth
12/7: septimal major sixth
13/7: 16/3-tone
2/1: octave

I have already described harmonics 8 to 16, but here is some more info and a chart showing its ratios. This scale sounds great when skillfully played and contains very good intervals (except for the ones with 7, 11 or 13 in their ratios). Remember that every second interval will be harmonics 4 to 8 and every fourth one will be harmonics 2 to 4. If you play harmonics 4 to 8 you will have only 4 tones. These make a harmonic major seventh chord. Although the 7/4 interval is a bit odd on its own, when you play the full chord it actually has a very powerful sound.

Harmonics 8 to 16

1/1: unison, perfect prime
9/8: major whole tone
5/4: major third
11/8: undecimal semi-augmented fourth
3/2: perfect fifth
13/8: tridecimal neutral sixth
7/4: harmonic seventh
15/8: classic major seventh
2/1: octave

Harmonics 9 to 18 have an amazing eastern sound that is great to play. They have a few odd intervals, but they also have a few very good sounding ones.

Harmonics 9 to 18:

1/1: unison, perfect prime
10/9: minor whole tone
11/9: undecimal neutral third
4/3: perfect fourth
13/9: tridecimal diminished fifth
14/9: septimal minor sixth
5/3: major sixth, BP sixth
16/9: Pythagorean minor seventh
17/9: septendecimal major seventh
2/1: octave

I have already described harmonics 10 to 20 as well, but here it is again with its ratios. Remember that harmonics 10 to 20 contain that amazing harmonic minor scale with very small magic numbered ratios.

Harmonics 10 to 20:

1/1: unison, perfect prime
11/10: 4/5-tone, Ptolemy's second
6/5: minor third
13/10: tridecimal semi-diminished fourth
7/5: septimal or Huygens' tritone, BP fourth
3/2: perfect fifth
8/5: minor sixth
17/10: septendecimal diminished seventh
9/5: just minor seventh, BP seventh
19/10: undevicesimal major seventh
2/1: octave

Harmonics 11 to 22 don't sound very good at all. "Disjointed" is the best word that comes to mind when I hear this scale. As you can see, all of the ratios are quite large and all have the number 11 in them. Two of them are so odd that they don't even have names. You can see that most of these names have the word "undecimal" in them. In mathematics the word undecimal means relating to the number 11. It is best to avoid undecimal intervals, as they really do sound quite bad.

Harmonics 11 to 22:

1/1: unison, perfect prime
12/11: 3/4-tone, undecimal neutral second
13/11: tridecimal minor third
14/11: undecimal diminished fourth or major third
15/11: undecimal augmented fourth
16/11: undecimal semi-diminished fifth
17/11:
18/11: undecimal neutral sixth
19/11:
20/11: large minor seventh
21/11: undecimal major seventh
2/1: octave

I already described harmonics 12 to 24 as being very nice to play. This scale is actually well recommended because it has 12 tones, and so is easy to play on a normal keyboard.

Harmonic 12 to 24:

1/1: unison, perfect prime
13/12: tridecimal 2/3-tone
7/6: septimal minor third
5/4: major third
4/3: perfect fourth
17/12: septendecimal tritone
3/2: perfect fifth
19/12: undevicesimal minor sixth
5/3: major sixth, BP sixth
7/4: harmonic seventh
11/6: 21/4-tone, undecimal neutral seventh
23/12: vicesimotertial major seventh
2/1: octave

Harmonics 13 to 26 sound very bad. Somehow, all of the notes manage to sound flat in relation to each other. The key word here is "tridecimal" (relating to 13). This scale is so weird that 5 of the intervals have no names.

Harmonics 13 to 26

1/1: unison, perfect prime
14/13: 2/3-tone
15/13: tridecimal 5/4-tone
16/13: tridecimal neutral third
17/13:
18/13: tridecimal augmented fourth
19/13:
20/13: tridecimal semi-augmented fifth
21/13:
22/13: tridecimal major sixth
23/13:
24/13: tridecimal neutral seventh
25/13:
2/1: octave

14 is an octave of 7, so I will skip it and move to 15. Harmonics 15 to 30 have some odd intervals, but they also have some very good ones with nice small ratios. Just as the fairly large 15 Hz and its octave 60 Hz were surprisingly good reference pitches for the Ptolemy scale, and the classic major seventh (15/8) was a surprisingly useful interval, so the harmonic scale associated with 15 also sounds surprisingly good.

Harmonics 15 to 30:

1/1: unison, perfect prime
16/15: minor diatonic semitone
17/15: septendecimal whole tone
6/5: minor third
19/15: undevicesimal ditone
4/3: perfect fourth
7/5: septimal or Huygens' tritone, BP fourth
22/15: undecimal diminished fifth
23/15:
8/5: minor sixth
5/3: major sixth, BP sixth
26/15: tridecimal semi-augmented sixth
9/5: just minor seventh, BP seventh
28/15: grave major seventh
29/15:
2/1: octave

The pattern seems to be clear; harmonic scales based on 7, 11, and 13 are very strange to play as they have no nice fifths, fourths, major thirds etc. while scales based on the other whole numbers from 1 to 15 are quite playable and all have a few good intervals in them. Having a scale with a few good intervals and some odd ones is fine, as odd notes are sometimes nice to play between really good ones. It is only when a scale has only odd intervals, as the ones based on 7, 11 and 13 do, that it becomes almost impossible to play in a way that actually sounds nice.

Because the best intervals don't have numbers larger than 16 in their ratios, I have only really explored the whole numbers from 1 to 16 fully. If we look at the numbers 16 to 32, ignoring octaves of 1 to 16 however, the next numbers to learn about would be 17, 19, 21, 23, 25, 27, 29 and 31. We already know that 432 Hz (octave of 27) is connected to the good numbers. 400 Hz (octave of 25) is also connected and can be found in the Ptolemy scale with 240 Hz (octave of 15) as its reference pitch.

When 400 Hz is used as a reference pitch the scale will actually contain some of the original 7 magic numbers, so 25, 50, 100, 200, 400 etc. are really magic numbers, too.

Ptolemy scale with 200 Hz as a reference pitch:

0: 200.000000 Hertz.
1: 213.333333 Hertz
2: 225.000000 Hertz
3: 240.000000 Hertz
4: 250.000000 Hertz
5: 266.666667 Hertz
6: 280.000000 Hertz
7: 300.000000 Hertz
8: 320.000000 Hertz
9: 333.333333 Hertz
10: 360.000000 Hertz
11: 375.000000 Hertz
12: 400.000000 Hertz

336 Hz (octave of 21) is also connected to the good numbers. You will find it in the Ptolemy scale when you use octaves of 7 Hz, 15 Hz or 268.8 Hz as its reference pitch (see charts in previous chapter). If you delve into those charts, however, you will see that it always related to the other magic numbers via the odd sounding seventh harmonic or the 7/5 devils interval...

The other numbers, 17, 19, 23, 29 and 31 don't seem to connect to the magic numbers at all, and don't sound good in ratios because they are too large, so I don't know much about them. What I have noticed, however, is that the numbers that don't connect well (7, 11, 13, 17, 19, 23, 29, 31) are all consecutive prime numbers...

Harmonic number patterns

When you start the harmonic series with different octaves of the magic numbers in this book, you will uncover even more patterns. The harmonic series for 18 Hz (octave of 9 Hz) and 24 Hz (octave of 3 Hz) in the following two images are good examples of this.

18	36	72	144	288
				306
			162	324
				342
		90	180	360
				378
			198	396
				414
	54	108	216	432
				450
			234	468
				504
		126	252	522
				540
			270	558
				576

If you use that numerology trick to break each number down in the above image to a single digit, 18 would be 9 because 1 + 8 = 9 and 36 would also be 9 because 3 + 6 = 9. All of the other numbers in the harmonic series for 18 Hz will do the same thing; they will all add up to 9. You can start the harmonic series with any number that adds up to 9, and all of the new numbers will do the same. If you do the same thing with the harmonic series for 24 Hz (following image) you get a repeating pattern of 6 - 3 - 9 - 6 - 3 - 9 - 6 - 3 - 9. If you want 3 - 6 - 9 just start the series with 3 or 12.

24	48	96	192	384
				408
			216	432
				456
		120	240	480
				504
			264	528
				552
	72	144	288	576
				600
			312	624
				648
		168	336	672
				672
			360	720
				744

Solfeggio tones, 440 Hz and the eleventh harmonic

If you look at the green blocks in the two previous charts you will see 396 Hz in the harmonic series for 18 Hz, and 528 Hz in the harmonic series for 24 Hz. These numbers are part of a set of frequencies called the "Solfeggio scale". The full set is: 171 - 417 - 741 - 285 - 528 - 852 - 396 - 639 - 963, with 528 Hz being known as the "love frequency". Unfortunately they mostly sound horrible together and are not very good for making music at all. You also won't find these numbers in any ancient text or anything like that, only on websites quoting a certain "Dr. H".

I think that the real Solfeggio scale is more likely to be the "do - re - mi - fa - SOL - la – ti" scale; the word SOL seems to hold a small clue… The only interesting place I have ever found these numbers is on every number pad in the world. Although they do represent the first 9 harmonics, the way the scale uses different arrangements of the numbers in each vertical row makes no harmonic sense.

What is really interesting, however, is that the green blocks on which 396 and 528 fell in the previous charts represent an "undecimal semi-augmented fourth" with a ratio of 11/8. This ratio represents the eleventh harmonic with its root raised by 3 octaves. I find it very interesting how these two solfeggio frequencies are off-set from octaves of 3 Hz and 9 Hz by this very unpleasant interval.

1	2	4	8	16 Octave
				17 17th harmonic
			9	18 Major whole tone
				19 19th harmonic
		5	10	20 Major third
				21 Narrow fourth
			11	22 Undecimal semi-augmented fourth
				23 23rd harmonic
3	6		12	24 Perfect fifth
				25 Classic augmented fifth
			13	26 Tridecimal neutral sixth
				27 Pythagorean major sixth
	7		14	28 Harmonic seventh
				29 29th harmonic
			15	30 Classic major seventh
				31 31st harmonic

I actually read an article in which scientists claim to have shattered cancer cells by playing two tones; a root tone matching the resonant frequency of the cancer cells and its eleventh harmonic (Google cancer and the 11th harmonic). This does not mean that the eleventh harmonic is healing; it means that it damages things.

There was already a chart earlier in this book that showed the Ptolemy scale with 11 Hz, or rather its higher octave of 352 Hz as its reference pitch. If you were awake you may have noticed that the solfeggio tones 396 Hz and 528 Hz, and also our modern day standard reference pitch A = 440 Hz, were in it. Here is a better chart highlighting this. It shows harmonics 16 to 32, but the relevant intervals are the same as in the Ptolemy scale. Because these intervals are directly from the harmonics series, you now know that 396 Hz, 440 Hz and 528 Hz are all harmonics of 11 Hz.

1/1	352	Unison, perfect prime
17/16	374	17th harmonic
9/8	396	Major whole tone
19/16	418	19th harmonic
5/4	440	Major third
21/16	462	Narrow fourth
11/8	484	Undecimal semi-augmented fourth
23/16	506	23rd harmonic
3/2	528	Perfect fifth
25/16	550	Classic augmented fifth
13/8	572	Tridecimal neutral sixth
27/16	594	Pythagorean major sixth
7/4	616	Harmonic seventh
29/16	638	29th harmonic
15/8	660	Classic major seventh
31/16	682	31st harmonic

You may remember that 11 Hz and its octaves don't share any harmonics with the magic frequencies, and that tones with no shared harmonics don't sound good together. This means that music with 396 Hz, 440 Hz or 528 Hz as reference pitches will not sound good with music that has the magic numbers like 256 Hz, 288 Hz, 384 Hz or 432 Hz as reference pitches, and so will not be good on the same album or in the same DJ mix.

Harmonic geometry

The harmonic series plays a major role not only in vibration but also in certain static shapes and forms. The Fibonacci series is the best place to start explaining this.

Fibonacci series

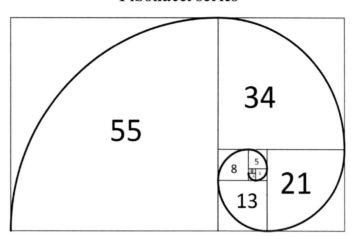

The Fibonacci series is a sequence of numbers that occurs frequently in nature. It can be seen in the arrangement of petals and seeds on flowers, in the spiral shape of snail shells and in the arrangement of branches and leaves on trees. It is the same spiral seen when water goes down a plug hole or when a hurricane forms around its eye, just as it is the same shape found in the spirals of galaxies and the hair on the tops of people's heads.

Man has used the Fibonacci series to copy nature for centuries. You will find it in the structure of many ancient buildings like the Parthenon in Greece, the Great Pyramids of Giza, Stonehenge, and also in the arrangement of some classical music where an 8 minute piece will often peak at 5 minutes. It is still used today by musicians, architects and artists to produce beautiful proportions that resonate with nature.

As a number sequence, the Fibonacci series becomes easy to understand. You just take the number one and add it to itself to get two. Then add them together to get three: 1 + 1 = 2 and 1 + 2 = 3. Now you have 1 - 2 - 3.

Then just add the last two numbers together to get the next number: 2 + 3 = 5. That gives you 1 - 1 - 2 - 3 - 5, add the last two numbers again, 3 + 5 = 8 and so you can go on and on. The result will be 1 - 1 - 2 - 3 - 5 - 8 - 13 - 21 - 34 - 55 - 89 - 144 ... it goes on forever, an infinite spiral growing exponentially larger with each new number.

If you take any two Fibonacci numbers that are next to each other, for example 5 and 8, and use them as lengths for the sides of a rectangle, you will get a golden rectangle with the golden ratio across its long and short sides. You will find the same ratio if you look at the double spiral of the seeds in some sunflowers, where if one side has 13 seeds the other will often have 21 (two sequential numbers from the Fibonacci series). You will find this pattern in the petals, leaves, seeds or other parts of many other plants like pine cones and pineapples, not only sunflowers.

You will also find the golden ratio in the perfectly proportioned pentagram; the circles in the image below show you the points where it is found in each long side.

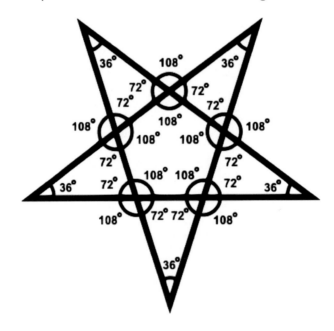

If you use the degrees in the angles of a pentagram as Hz, you will find that 36 Hz to 72 Hz is an octave and 72 Hz to 108 Hz is a perfect fifth.

1	D	36
		Octave
2	D	72
		Fifth
3	A	108

These are the first three harmonics in the harmonic series for 36 Hz, and are also all that the Pythagorean scale is made of (octaves and perfect fifths). Now I can see why the Pythagoreans liked this symbol so much.

If you take the last digit in the first 60 Fibonacci numbers you will find a pattern of numbers that repeats through the entire infinite series, starting again after every 60 numbers and repeating in their last digits. If you arrange these 60 numbers in rows with 5 numbers in each one as I have below, a pattern of 0, 5, 5, 0, 5, 5... reveals itself in the first row. There are many similar hidden patterns to be found in the Fibonacci series when you play with it mathematically, which is why mathematicians are still studying it.

0, 1, 1, 2, 3,
5, 8, 3, 1, 4,
5, 9, 4, 3, 7,
0, 7, 7, 4, 1,
5, 6, 1, 7, 8,
5, 3, 8, 1, 9,
0, 9, 9, 8, 7,
5, 2, 7, 9, 6,
5, 1, 6, 7, 3,
0, 3, 3, 6, 9,
5, 4, 9, 3, 2,
5, 7, 2, 9, 1.

If you raise the Fibonacci series by a few octaves to get musical tones, you will find the octave and a fifth needed to make a Pythagorean scale right at the start (1-2-3). You will also find a C major chord with a 5/4 major third and a 3/2 perfect fifth. This is the same chord found in the Ptolemy scale and in the harmonic series, only the order of the notes and the octaves they are in is different. This kind of chord is called an inverted chord. A normal major chord would be 256 Hz - 320 Hz - 384 Hz, while this one is 256 Hz - 384 Hz - 640 Hz. The general feeling of the chord is the same as the original, though.

Fibonacci series				
C	C	G	E	C
1	2	3	5	8
2	4	6	10	16
4	8	12	20	32
8	16	24	40	64
16	32	48	80	128
32	64	96	160	256
64	128	192	320	512
128	256	384	640	1024
Major chord				

In the image below I have done the same thing with the harmonic series. As you can see, it contains the same octave and fifth and also the same C major chord, only the notes in the chord are in the correct order. This connection between the harmonic and Fibonacci series actually is pretty obvious. The Fibonacci series = 1-1-2-3-5-8-13… and the harmonic series = 1-2-3-4-5-6-7-8-9-10-11-12-13… So, the harmonic series really contains the entire Fibonacci series within its sequence numbers.

Harmonic series					
C	C	G	C	E	G
1	2	3	4	5	6
2	4	6	8	10	12
4	8	12	16	20	24
8	16	24	32	40	48
16	32	48	64	80	96
32	64	96	128	160	192
64	128	192	256	320	384
				Major chord	

In the above chart you can see that this major chord is found between harmonics 4, 5, and 6 in the harmonic series. The numbers 4, 5, and 6 actually reveal its structure and ratios: 5/4 = a major third, 6/5 = a minor third and 6/4 can be lowered to 3/2 which is a perfect fifth. So, this chord is really a 5/4 major third with a 6/5 minor third on top of it, and these add up to make a 3/2 perfect fifth.

The 12 tone Ptolemy scale has this 4-5-6 major chord when played in its root key, and it also has a 6/5 minor third in its root key just below the major third (as on any piano). So, you can play a major or minor chord in the root key of this scale and it will still mirror the geometry in this chapter, only the minor chord inverts things somewhat.

Pythagorean Theorem

The same major chord shows up in the Pythagorean theorem. This theorem states that *a* squared + *b* squared = *c* squared. In other words, the sum of the squares of two sides of a right triangle is equal to the square of the hypotenuse. This theorem is used in theoretical mathematics and also in real world calculations. An obvious example would be calculating the exact length of a ramp when you only know the height (*a*) and distance on flat ground (*b*).

Image by: Florin De Gelder

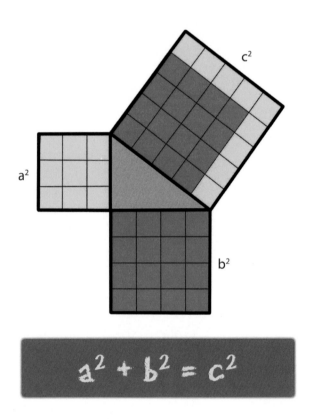

$$a^2 + b^2 = c^2$$

When I first saw the above image, I noticed that there are 3, 4, and 5 cubes in each side of the triangle. I was not sure if this was just art or if they were actual ratios. So, I used Google's Pythagorean theorem calculator and found that 2 squared + 3 squared really does = 5 squared. Because 3, 4, and 5 are octaves of 192 Hz, 256 Hz and 320 Hz, I figured that it should be the same with them. After checking with Google I found that I was right: If *a* = 192 Hz, and *b* = 256 Hz then *c* = 320 Hz. This is the exact same 4-5-6 major chord found in "everything", only it is inverted with 6 being lowered by an octave to 3.

The tetractys is another important Pythagorean symbol. It consists of ten points arranged with 1, 2, 3 and 4 points in each row to make a perfect equilateral triangle.

Tetractys

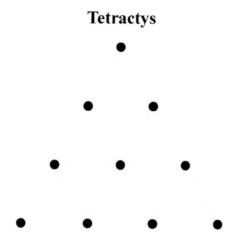

Musically, it represents the first 4 harmonics which contain the favorite ancient Greek intervals: the octave, the perfect fifth and the perfect fourth in the spaces between them.

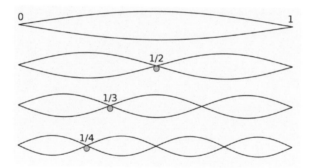

To the Pythagoreans the numbers 1 to 4 had cosmic meanings. These seem to mirror the sonic properties of the intervals connected to them quite well.

No	Meaning	Interval	Ratio
1	Unity	Fundamental	1/1
2	Power	Octave	2/1
3	Harmony	Perfect fifth	3/2
4	Cosmos	Perfect fourth	4/3

The tetractys also represented space:

1 = a single point with no dimensions.

2 = one dimension (a line between two points).

3 = two dimensions (a flat triangle with 3 points).

4 = three dimensions (a tetrahedron with 4 points).

The Pythagoreans actually had a prayer about the tetractys:

"Bless us, divine number, thou who generated gods and men! O holy, holy Tetractys, thou that containest the root and source of the eternally flowing creation! For the divine number begins with the profound, pure unity until it comes to the holy four; then it begets the mother of all, the all-comprising, all-bounding, the first-born, the never-swerving, the never-tiring holy ten, the keyholder of all."

When initiates joined the Pythagoreans they had to take an oath, which also mentioned the tetractys:

"By that pure, holy, four lettered name on high,

nature's eternal fountain and supply,

the parent of all souls that living be,

by him, with faith find oath, I swear to thee."

Regular polygons

But this is not the end of the story; the harmonic series is found in many more places throughout the geometric world. If, for example, you take the degrees in the interior angles of the regular polygons and add the numbers of the angles in each one together, or take the amount of degrees in the circles in the flower of life, you will find it in both of them.

How this works: An equilateral triangle has 60 degrees in each corner, so 60 x 3 = 180 degrees. A square has 90 degrees in each corner, so 90 x 4 = 360 degrees and so on (note that the tetractys also forms a perfect equilateral triangle).

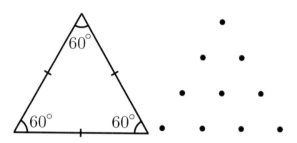

Harmonic geometry			
Note	Harmonic	Degrees in all angles added together	Degrees in Flower of life
F#	1	180 = Triangle (60 x 3)	360 = 1 circle
F#	2	360 = Square (90 x 4)	720 = 2 circles
C#	3	540 = Pentagon (108 x 5)	1080 = 3 circles
F#	4	720 = Hexagon (120 x 6)	1440 = 4 circles
A#	5	900 = Septagon (128.571428 x 7)	1800 = 5 circles
C#	6	1080 = Octagon (135 x 8)	2160 = 6 circles
E	7	1260 = Nonagon (140 x 9)	2520 = 7 circles

180-360-540-720-900-1080-2160 = harmonic series for 180 Hz (regular polygons).

360-720-1080-1440-1800-2160-2520 = harmonic series for 360 Hz (flower of life).

360 Hz is one octave above 180 Hz so they are octaves of the same note, which happens to be F# in the Ptolemy scale when it has 384 Hz as its reference pitch.

As you can see there is a 4-5-6 F# major chord between F#, A# and C#. The ratios in this chord are the same as in the 4-5-6 major chord earlier in this chapter, only here it is in F# instead of G. Obviously it does not matter what key you play it in, the ratios and geometry will always be the same.

Platonic solids

Plato's 3 dimensional Platonic solids are also made of these shapes. If you take the degrees in their interior angles and add the numbers together you get this:

Tetrahedron = 5 equilateral triangles = 720 degrees

Hexahedron (cube) = 6 squares = 2160 degrees.

Octahedron = 8 equilateral triangles= 1440 degrees

Dodecahedron = 12 pentagons = 6480 degrees

Icosahedron = 20 equilateral triangles = 3600 degrees.

Plato also connected these to the 5 elements:

Tetrahedron = Fire

Hexahedron (cube) = Earth

Octahedron = Air

Dodecahedron = Aether

Icosahedron = Water

What is quite interesting is that if you take the degrees for the 4 Earthly ones (leave out aether) and add them together you get 7920, which is very close to the diameter of the Earth in miles (Earth diameter = 7917.5 miles). To add to this, the moon's diameter is about 2160 miles which is the same number as the amount of degrees in a cube. I don't know what this means but there are more similar examples involving the Sun, Earth and Moon in the next chapter, so it is not an isolated thing.

It is also worth noting that with each number in the degrees of the pentagram, the flower of life, the regular polygons and the platonic solids (when their angles are added together) you will find that they all break down to 9 when their digits are added together to make a single one.

The basic building blocks here (triangle, square, pentagon etc.) all connect mathematically to the harmonic series which is amazing. But it gets better, as they can be connected to it physically, too. To better understand this we need to look at cymatics.

Cymatics

People who work with cymatics stimulate various substances like sand or water with sound, and observe the patterns that are created. This was first discovered in the west by a German physicist and musician named Ernst Chladni who found that drawing a violin bow across a metal plate with sand on it would cause the sand to make amazing patterns. He found that drawing the bow at different speeds and angles would cause the plate to vibrate at its fundamental pitch or various harmonics of this, causing nodal patterns that got more complex with higher harmonics. Ancient Chinese gong makers knew about this and would hang gongs horizontally and use sand cymatics to see where the gong needed more hammering. It is said that the masters knew secret patterns for the best resonance, but this knowledge is mostly lost in the sands of time now.

These days people just play a tone from a tone generator and use a transducer (very strong speaker) to vibrate the metal plate. When they use a tone generator and move the pitch around, they find that certain frequencies make really nice patterns while others do not. Just as Chladni found, lower ones make simple patterns while higher ones make more complex ones. Many people make the mistake of assuming that these frequencies are healing or special in some way, when they are really just the plate's resonant frequency and its harmonics.

To really understand cymatics you need to remove the plate, as its shape influences the shape of the patterns too much. To see this in action you really should watch a short video on YouTube called "Shape oscillation of a levitated drop in an acoustic field". In this video they have taken a transducer and aimed it at a reflector so that the sound bounces back at it. This creates a standing wave with pockets of high and low air pressure that are fixed in place and don't move at all. When this happens you can place small objects or drops of water in these pockets and they will float in the air! This is called "sonic levitation" and there are many videos about it online.

But in the "Shape oscillation of a levitated drop in an acoustic field" video they do something amazing. They play the fundamental frequency of the drop of water, and it flattens into a disk (circle). Then they play the second harmonic (octave) of this pitch and it becomes elongated, like a sausage. This sausage, however, is oscillating. The ends move together and the sides move apart, forming new ends so that it was like a "plus symbol" but with only one line visible at a time, at the peak of each oscillation. When they play the third harmonic the water forms a triangle, also oscillating with another one so that both together would be a Star of David, but only one was fully formed at a time.

And so they go on. Each harmonic's shape has the same amount of sides as its sequence number; 1 = circle, 2 = sausage, 3 = triangle, 4 = square, 5 = pentagon and so on. The video stops after a few harmonics, but if you carry on you will eventually have so many sides that you will have what appears to be a circle again, only it won't actually be one.

I find this to be of extreme interest, as each harmonic's sequence number now also has a physical shape. Obviously cymatics made using metal plates and other objects are just showing you complex versions of these basic shapes, made so by the extra factors being brought in by the objects' physical properties. All cymatic patterns become more complex with higher frequencies, so this must be what is going on.

The Ptolemy and Pythagorean scales in this book are made from the same ratios found in these shapes, and the equal temperament scale is closely based on them. So, all in all, it seems like the saying "geometry is frozen music" is far more accurate than some would believe.

Music of the spheres

Since frequencies are measured in Hz (cycles per second), knowing how the second was made should be important history to any musician. Some people say that the second is just a random man-made measure. Well, it is man-made but it is not random at all. The second was first defined as 1/86.400 of one solar day, and later in terms of the Earth's orbit around the sun. Nowadays it is measured using atomic clocks that use the transitional rate of certain atoms to define the second. This new second is not really different to the older solar based one, only more stable (the Earth changes speed now and again). I think it is nice to know that the second is based on an equal division of a solar day, and that it really is a cosmic measure by the very definition of the word.

To find out more about time, I went to Google's unit converters (seconds to hours, hours to days etc.). I started with a 12 hour half day. This represents exactly half a turn in the Earth's rotation. I was quite blown away to find that there were exactly 43200 seconds in 12 hours. This actually makes perfect sense because the second was first defined as 1/86.400 of one solar day, and 43200 x 2 = 86400...

The following chart tracks 25920 years of time. While making it I realized that I could just use the mathematics from the harmonic series. If you look at the column furthest to the right in each part of the chart, you will see 1, 2, 3, 4, 5, 6, 7 etc. This harmonic structure is mirrored in all of the numbers to the left of them. I guess this is all kind of obvious...

I used 28 day lunar months instead on normal ones because they make much more sense. If you like this idea, you can download 28 day 13 month lunar calendars online. With this system there are 364 days instead of 365, so these calendars add one holiday to make 365 days. Pure mathematics never really fits into nature perfectly, even our 365 days in a year is not really accurate, there are actually closer to 365.2422 days in a year. And the moon really takes about 27 days, 7 hours, 43 minutes, 11.6 seconds to orbit the Earth once, not 28. These orbits and rotations are also always modulating and changing speed, so there are really no accurate numbers for any of this. Basically the ancient people who first came up with this seem to have used harmonic mathematics, and somehow came up with a system that fits with the actual movements suspiciously well.

Seconds	Minutes	Hours	Days	Weeks	Lunar months	Years	Planet movements
60	1						
120	2						
180	3						
240	4						
300	5						
360	6						
420	7						
480	8						
540	9						
600	10						
660	11						
720	12						
1440	24...						

Seconds	Minutes	Hours	Days	Weeks	Lunar months	Years	Planet movements
3600	60	1					
7200	120	2					
10800	180	3					
14400	240	4					
18000	300	5					
21600	360	6					
25200	420	7					
28800	480	8					
32400	540	9					
36000	600	10					
39600	660	11					
43200	720	12					Earth rotates 180 degrees

Seconds	Minutes	Hours	Days	Weeks	Lunar months	Years	Planet movements
86400	1440	24	1				Earth rotates 360 degrees
172800	2880	48	2				
259200	4320	72	3				
345600	5760	96	4				
432000	7200	120	5				
518400	8640	144	6				
604800	10080	168	7	1			
	20160	336	14	2			
	30240	504	21	3			

From this point I have left out some of the very long numbers on the left.

Seconds	Minutes	Hours	Days	Weeks	Lunar months	Years	Planet movements
		672	28	4	1		Moon orbits earth once
		1344	56	8	2		
		2016	84	12	3		
		2688	112	16	4		
		3360	140	20	5		
		4032	168	24	6		
		4704	196	28	7		
		5376	224	32	8		
		6048	252	36	9		
		6720	280	40	10		
		7392	308	44	11		
		8064	336	48	12		

Seconds	Minutes	Hours	Days	Weeks	Lunar months	Years	Planet movements
		8736	364	52	13	1	Earth orbits the sun once
			728	104	26	2	
			1092	156	39	3	
			1456	208	52	4	
			1820	260	65	5	
			2184	312	78	6	
			2548	364	91	7	
			2912	416	104	8	
			3276	468	117	9	
			3640	520	130	10	
			4004	572	143	11	
			4368	624	156	12	

Seconds	Minutes	Hours	Days	Weeks	Lunar months	Years	Planet movements
							Earth moves though:
					864	72	One degree in the zodiac
					25920	2160	30 degrees / One zodiac age
						25920	12 zodiacal ages (1 great year)

The bottom 3 rows in the above chart are of particular interest to me. In case you don't know, our Earth wobbles on its axis much like a spinning top often does. This causes the stars in the sky to shift very slightly to one side every night. It takes about 72 years for them to shift by only one degree and about 2160 years to shift 30 degrees. 30 degrees x 12 = 360 degrees or one full wobble, so each 30 degree arc has been connected to one of the 12 zodiac signs / constellations in the night sky. The full 360 degree wobble takes about 25920 years to complete and move through all 12 signs (2160 x 12 = 25920). This large cycle is called a "great year".

Since ancient times there have been people who believe that this cycle causes "light" and "dark" spiritual ages on Earth. Right now we are said to be transitioning from the Pisces to the

Aquarian age, which is meant to be a very spiritual age. Because each age lasts about 2160 years, however, nobody seems to know the exact date of the change.

There are many magic numbers that show up in our measures of time and in the music scales in this book. I am sure you are getting to know and recognize them by now. The reason why the same numbers show up in both places may actually be quite simple; all of them are harmonically connected to the number 1. Our measures of time are harmonically based on 1 second, which is based on one full rotation of the Earth. And the notes in the scales are also harmonically connected to the number 1 or 1 Hz (1 cycle per second).

Seconds	Minutes	Hours	Days	Planet movements
60	1			
3600	60	1		
43200	720	12		
86400	1440	24	1	Earth rotates once

This may seem like a good explanation, but when you look at the sizes and distances between the Sun, Earth and Moon, all logic has to go out of the window. The distance from the Sun to the Earth, for example, is about 108 times the diameter of the Sun, and the distance from the Earth to the Moon is about 108 times the diameter of the Moon. Also the Moon's diameter is about 2160 miles and its radius is about 1080 miles, while the Sun's diameter is about 864000 miles and its radius is about 432000 miles. If you remove the 0's at the ends of these numbers you get 108, 216, 432 and 864, which are all octaves of 432. Each 0 = the tenth harmonic, which is a major third + 3 octaves, so there is a strange harmonic symmetry between all of these numbers.

Another crazy thing is that the sun and moon are only the same size in the sky from Earth because the sun's diameter is about 400 times greater than the moon, and the sun is also about 400 times farther away (400 is also a magic number). This is what makes total eclipses possible on Earth. The moon also orbits the Earth is such a way that the same side always faces us, while the other "dark side" always faces away.

Each of the above things could be explained if they were on their own, but all of them together are just too much to put neatly in a box. Even if these are all approximate measures, all of them being so close is still quite profound. If you are wondering how close they are, the Sun's size and the Earth's rotation are not constant and these are actually the official estimates. The moon's diameter is said to be closer to 2159 than 2160 and its radius closer to 1079 than 1080, so we are within 1 mile of accuracy with that.

The most logical explanation I can think of is that some god level being or beings designed these planets using mathematics, but that is quite a thing to say without any proof. If this is the case, however, the math would actually have been very simple:

432 x 100 = 43200 seconds (12 hours)
432 x 200 = 86400 seconds (24 hours) (one rotation of the earth)
432 x 60 = 25920 years (one great year)
432 x 5 = 2160 miles (Moons diameter)
432 x 2.5 = 1080 miles (Moons radius)
432 x 2000 = 864000 miles (Suns diameter)
432 x 1000 = 432000 miles (Suns radius)

Bonus fact: 432 x 432 = 186624 (Speed of light = about 186000 miles per second in a vacuum).

One thing worth noting is that these patterns only show up in the imperial measures of inches, feet, yards or miles, while metric measures like cm or km for distance don't reveal much of anything. I guess the imperial system must have some ancient connections that I don't know about yet. How all of this came to be is beyond my understanding, but since this timeless mathematical system is also the best one for low decimal scale making, it seems like we are stuck with it.

You may have noticed the number 432 or 4320, 43200, 432000 etc. in most of the scales, and in the mathematics behind many other things in this book. This is interesting because there are many people who swear that music tuned around A = 432 Hz is really good to listen to. If you take into account that 432 Hz is in vibrational harmony with the average rotation speed and movements of the Earth, it makes me wonder if this might not actually be true.

I mentioned before that on a piano you can make a key ring by hitting the key an octave + a fifth below it, and that this works because the lower key has the higher one as its second harmonic. I also mentioned how this works with equal temperament, even though the notes are slightly out of tune. This means that even if the rotation and movements of the Earth change speed slightly according to other cycles, playing music that is tuned to the estimated average should still "connect" quite well. Although there is no physical proof that frequencies vibrating in approximate harmony with the rotation speed of the Earth are better for you to listen to, creating art, making music or constructing buildings to mirror the heavens and its cycles has still been done for thousands of years, hence the saying "as above so below".

Most of the ancient cultures like the Egyptians, Mayans, Sumerians etc. were obsessed with this, and built many of their important structures to align with various planets and cosmic events, especially the sunrise and sunset on the solstices. You can tell that most of them used "harmonic mathematics" by the numbers that you find in their measures.

A good example of this is the Great Pyramid of Giza. It is part of an arrangement of 3 pyramids set up to mirror the 3 stars in the constellation of Orion, and was originally covered with exactly 144000 casing stones. There are also many examples the golden ratio in its design, but the most interesting thing of all is that when you hit the kings "sarcophagus", the whole area echoes at around 108 Hz with a clear 432 Hz harmonic above it.

Another good example is Stonehenge in England. Its outer circle of stones is about 108 feet in diameter, and it is aligned to the sunset and sunrise on the solstices. A very interesting site to look into as well is Angor Wat in Cambodia. There are many examples of 432, 108, 144 etc. in the structures and statues there. For an amazing sight, type "Angor Wat" into Google Earth's search bar and see for yourself how it lines up with the lat / long grid for a perfect solstice alignment.

There are even some fairly modern cities and buildings that are still aligned with the solstices such as "Manhattanhenge" with its obelisk and aligned streets in New York, and the central oval obelisk area in the Vatican City (harmonic mathematics may have been used in the design of the Vatican City as it occupies exactly 108 acres of land). Both of these obelisks were originally from ancient Egypt and were brought to the west with great effort and at great cost. These are not the only obelisks that made this long journey; there are two more, one in London and another in Paris. This adds up to 4 obelisks in 4 of the modern world's greatest power centers that were brought from the old power center of the world where our culture began. I recently read an article which stated that the "Institute of Digital Archaeology" wants to install Temple of Baal archway replicas in Times Square in New York City and in Trafalgar Square in London, so I guess these people still exist...

The same numbers turn up in many religions. Yogis, for example, have strings of beads called "Shiva beads" that always come on strings with 108 beads, while on New Year's Eve Buddhist temples in Japan ring their bells 108 times to remember the 108 human sins and worldly desires. The "Kali Yuga" also is an important long time cycle in some Indian religions that lasts for 432000 years. Even the Jehovah's witnesses seem to know something because they come right to my door and tell me that exactly 144000 people will be chosen by God to save the world one day.

The Mayan's used the same maths in their famous measures of time, in their time cycles; 1 Tun = 360 days, 1 Katun = 7200 days and 1 Baktun = 144000 days. The Sumerians also used it for all kinds of things, with numbers like 12 and 60 being used for time and 360 for geometry... There are many more examples, but I will stop here.

It could be that just as I found certain numbers to be the best for getting a low decimal count, so other people throughout the ages also found the same numbers to be the most useful for making big calculations and measurements with minimal decimals. If they used this type of harmonic based system, then they would always have ended up with "magic" numbers like 4320 or 1440. The following image of the Ptolemy scale with 360 Hz as its reference pitch goes into the higher octaves. In it you can see how numbers like 4320, 1440, 14400, 19200 and even 25920 (great year) are in the scale. This can only mean that a similar mathematical system was used.

360 Hz Ptolemy / Just intonation										
F#	1/1	90	180	360	720	1440	2880	5760	11520	23040
G	16/15	96	192	384	768	1536	3072	6144	12288	24576
G#	9/8	101.25	202.5	405	810	1620	3240	6480	12960	25920
A	6/5	108	216	432	864	1728	3456	6912	13824	27648
A#	5/4	112.5	225	450	900	1800	3600	7200	14400	28800
B	4/3	120	240	480	960	1920	3840	7680	15360	30720
C	7/5	126	252	504	1008	2016	4032	8064	16128	32256
C#	3/2	135	270	540	1080	2160	4320	8640	17280	34560
D	8/5	144	288	576	1152	2304	4608	9216	18432	36864
D#	5/3	150	300	600	1200	2400	4800	9600	19200	38400
E	9/5	162	324	648	1296	2592	5184	10368	20736	41472
F	15/8	168	336	672	1344	2688	5376	10752	21504	43008
F#	2/1	180	360	720	1440	2880	5760	11520	23040	46080

If you try and trace this all back, we had the ancient Greeks, Socrates and his students, Aristotle and Plato, then before them, also in Greece and a great influence on their work, we had Pythagoras who seems to have been the first to bring this knowledge to the west. Pythagoras is said to have traveled from Greece to Egypt to study in their mystery schools, after which he was captured by the Persians and sent to the city of Babylon in Mesopotamia which they had conquered and were ruling at the time. There he studied with the Chaldaeans of Babylon and the Magi of Persia before eventually returning to Greece with all of this information. The Babylonian and Assyrian / Syrian civilizations grew out of the ancient Sumerian civilization, which is said to be the first advanced human civilization on Earth. When you try to trace things further back than the Sumerians, you will enter the realms of the god level beings and will find versions of reality that very different to what we know.

What we do know for sure is that there must have been a huge global culture of pyramid / huge stone block builders that existed all around the world thousands of years ago, because the stones are mostly still there. We know that these people knew all about astronomy and were very good at mathematics, because of the way these structures were built. The strange thing about them is that the oldest ones often have the biggest stones and finest stone work. These ancient stones are sometimes so big that no human could ever have moved them, and they sometimes have gaps between them that are smaller than the width of a human hair. It is a fact that nobody really knows who made some of the oldest structures in Egypt, South America and many other places, and that some of the "ancient cultures" actually discovered but did not build all of them.

Why this timeline is important is because our culture has been heavily influenced by the Ancient Greeks who, in turn, were heavily influenced by the Egyptians, Babylonians, Sumerians and so on. Whether the first known human civilizations were pre-dated by other humans, aliens or god level beings is impossible to tell; nobody really knows what happened that long ago.

The one thing that is constant is this harmonic number system, this matrix of mystery that keeps popping up over and over again. I think these numbers are really the numbers of nature, expressing the path of least resistance mathematically.

The human body starts out as 1 cell, then 2-4-8-16-32 etc. (octaves)

Water down a plug hole / spiral galaxies = 1-1-2-3-5-8 etc. (Fibonacci series)

Most beat free intervals / sacred geometry = 1-2-3-4-5-6-7-8 etc. (Harmonic series)

All three of these things are represented by the simplest small whole number sequences, the same ones that the ratios and frequencies in this book are based on. This means that "harmonic mathematics" really does represent nature, as both follow the same most efficient path of least resistance to do things. When studied closely using sound, numbers that are closer to 1 are connected to more enlightening intervals, while things get more complex and emotional as you go further away from it. In the end it seems as if 1 is the true source of everything, the seed from which everything grows and the place to which everything returns...

How to tune synthesizers and instruments

By now you must really want to know how to implement this in real life, and how to tune actual instruments to exact Hz values. Remember that choirs naturally sing the perfect self-adapting scale with small ratios in any key, so the tuning systems in this book are only needed because we have instruments with fixed tuning that don't behave naturally...

The word we use for this is kind of tuning is "micro-tuning". With micro-tuning you can play Pythagorean, Ptolemy / just Intonation or any other scale you can think of. Many popular VST synthesizers can be tuned in this way. I use Omnisphere 2®, Kontakt 5®, Serum®, Zebra 2®, CrX 4®, Cronox 2 and Albino 3® together.

Equal temperament is the only fixed scale that sounds the same in any key, while Pythagorean and just intonation scales sound better in their root keys and certain other keys. So, the best choice of scale is really dependent on the type of music that you want to make. Equal temperament is best for music like jazz where the root key changes a lot, while the Ptolemy scale is best for music like deep house or psytrance where the root key stays the same most of the time.

For this reason you may find that when you make a full album, you might want to use different scales for each song. Because equal temperament is closely based on just intonation / Pythagorean tuning, you will find that using the same magic numbers as reference pitches for all 3 scales will result in good all round harmony between them. A is normally used as the reference note for equal temperament, so using A = 432 Hz will be a sensible option as a reference pitch for it.

In the following image you can see that equal temperament with A = 432 Hz has many notes that are within 1 Hz, or otherwise very close to the same notes in the Pythagorean scale with 432 Hz, and the Ptolemy scale with 384 Hz as reference pitches.

	432 equal temp	384 Ptolemy	432 Pythagorean
A	216.0000	216.0000	216.0000
A#	228.8440	230.4000	230.6601
B	242.4518	240.0000	243.0000
C	256.8687	256.0000	256.0000
C#	272.1429	268.8000	273.3750
D	288.3254	288.0000	288.0000
D#	305.4701	307.2000	307.5468
E	323.6343	320.0000	324.0000
F	342.8786	345.6000	345.9902
F#	363.2672	360.0000	364.5000
G	384.8682	384.0000	384.0000
G#	407.7537	409.6000	410.0625
A	432.0000	432.0000	432.0000

If you want to use the Ptolemy or Pythagorean scales then you should learn to use the amazing free scale making software called "Scala" which can be downloaded from this link: http://www.huygens-fokker.org/scala/index.html. There are also many tutorials, links and information on the Scala web page, so it is a very a good place to read and learn more about micro-tuning.

With Scala you can generate scales like Pythagorean, just intonation, harmonic, equal temperament, or make scales of your own. You can then export them in a variety of different formats like bulk dump midi files, .scl and .tun files that can be loaded into various hardware and software synthesizers to adjust each note individually.

How to use Scala

Even if you don't have any micro-tunable synthesizers, Scala has its own sound player and mouse operated keyboard. So, while reading the following tutorial, keep in mind that you can hit the "play" icon and listen to what you have loaded or generated at any time. You can also hit the "show" icon to get a nice readout of your scale as ratios, Hz, cents or other formats.

First I will explain how to make the scales and export them as various formats for various synths, and then I will explain how to load them into the synths. Obviously the first thing you need to do is download and install Scala on your computer. You can find this link: http://www.huygens-fokker.org/scala/downloads.html

For installation instructions on downloads for mac read this:
http://curtismacdonald.com/microtuning-midi/

On Windows you must also install gtk2-runtime-2.24.10-2012-10-10-ash.exe for Scala to work. This is the best link: http://gtk-win.sourceforge.net/home/index.php/Main/Downloads

Keep in mind that installation is very easy on a PC and very hard on mac.

To get the Pythagorean and Ptolemy scale pre-sets that I used in this book into Scala, you need to download the free zip file containing hundreds of scales from this link: http://www.huygens-fokker.org/scala/downloads.html

Unzip this zip file into the folder in your program files where you installed Scala.

These are the file names for the 3 scales you may want to try first.

"pyth_12.scl" (12 tone Pythagorean scale)

"ji_12.scl" (12 tone Ptolemy scale)

"ptolemy.scl" (7 tone Ptolemy scale)

The scales in the zip file are in the ".scl." format. They cannot be loaded into most synths, but they can be opened and edited in Scala. Then they can be exported in a variety of formats for various software and hardware synths. If you want to use one of the presets, follow the tutorial below but use "File" and "Open scale" to browse for your scale and load it. When it is loaded, continue from step 5.

If you want to generate a scale, just go to "file", "new" and "scale". There you will find some nice options to generate your own .scl files which you can then edit and convert to .tun or another format. If you select "harmonic scale" you will get a very nice 12 tone harmonic scale made from the 4th to 16th harmonics. You can change it to 16 to 32 or any other harmonic scale that you like. When you have chosen your scale hit "apply" and "ok", and continue from step 5 in the following tutorial.

To use a scale with more than 12 notes on a 12 tone keyboard you can edit it manually, choosing the 12 best sounding tones to make your own custom scale that best suits the music you are making. To edit the frequencies of the individual notes in a scale manually using charts from my book, just go to "edit" and "edit scale" then you can double click on any frequency and remove it, or enter a new one in its place. If you want to hear the scale before exporting, you can just click "play" on the bottom right, then when you click on a frequency in the chart it will play that note in the built in midi player. Don't forget to hit "apply" and "OK" afterwards.

If you want to make your own scale using Hz or ratios from the charts in this book, you can simply start with an empty scale and enter your notes or intervals one at a time. To do this, start on step 1 in the following tutorial:

1: Open Scala and go to "File" – "New" and select "Scale" or hold "Ctrl" and click "I" as a keyboard shortcut to do the same thing. This will open a new empty scale that only contains one note (perfect prime).

2: Double click the frequency of your perfect prime and change it to whatever frequency you want your reference pitch to be. If you are not sure where to start, here is the chart with those 12 really useful reference pitches again.

Note	Ratios	Hz frequencies over a few octaves	Bpm
G	1/1	192, 96, 48, 24, 12, 6, 3, 1.5	90 / 180
G#	16/15	102.4, 51.2, 25.6, 12.8, 6.4, 3.2, 1.6, 0.8, 0.4, 0.2, 0.1	96 / 192
A	9/8	216, 108, 54, 27, 13.5	50.625 / 101.25
A#	6/5	230.4, 115.2, 57.6, 28.8, 14.4, 7.2, 3.6, 1.8, 0.9	54 / 108
B	5/4	240, 120, 60, 30, 15, 7.5	56.25 / 112.5
C	4/3	256, 128, 64, 32, 16, 8, 4, 2, 1, 0.5	60 / 120
C#	7/5	268.8, 134.4, 67.2, 33.6, 16.8, 8.4, 4.2, 2.1	63 / 126
D	3/2	288, 144, 72, 36, 18, 9, 4.5	67.5 / 135
D#	8/5	307.2, 157.6, 76.8, 38.4, 19.2, 9.6, 4.8, 2.4, 1.2, 0.6, 0.3	72 / 144
E	5/3	320, 160, 80, 40, 20, 10, 5, 2.5	75 / 150
F	9/5	345.6, 172.8, 86.4, 43.2, 21.6, 10.8, 5.4, 2.7	81 / 162
F#	15/8	360, 180, 90, 45, 22.5	84. 375 / 168. 75

3: Now you can simply enter the data for each note in the white "new pitch" bar.

To enter a frequency as Hz, you have to add a "z" before your number. So, for 288 Hz you would enter "z288" and hit "enter".

To enter a ratio, just type it in. So, for a major third, just type 5/4 and hit "enter".

To enter a note using the amounts of cents that it is above perfect prime, just enter the numbers like this: 386.3137 (cents above perfect prime) and hit enter.

When you hit enter you will see your new note appear below "perfect prime". Continue like this, adding more notes until you have built one octave of your scale.

The last note in your scale must be an octave with a ratio of 2/1. You only need one octave because Scala generates the others for you, making a full scale that covers your whole keyboard. Obviously it works best if there are 12 notes in your scale, otherwise each octave will fall on a different note making the scale hard to play.

4: When your scale is ready, hit "Apply" and "OK" and click "show scale" under "view" in the main window to make sure your scale is loaded.

5: Go to "Edit" (top of main window) and click "preferences" right at the bottom of the "Edit" drop down menu. This will open the "User Options" window.

6: Click the top "Output" tab and make sure that your "base frequency" (reference pitch) is correct.

7: Click the "MIDI" tab (in the user options window) and change your "reference frequency" to match your base frequency.

8: Below "reference frequency", you can change "reference key" and "key for 1/1" to the correct note for your reference pitch.

9: Click on the "Synth" tab and select the correct synth under "tuning model". Most VST synths will use .tun files (112 in the drop down menu).

10: Click "Apply" and "Ok" then close the "User Options" window.

11: To save it as .scl, you must go "File" and "Save Scale As" and select ".scl"

12: To export your scale as .tun or another format, go to "File" and "Export Synth Tuning".

13: Select export destination and hit "Ok".

Your scale is now ready to load into your synthesizer.

Some synthesizers refuse to play the base frequency, playing all the notes perfectly except for the base frequency itself. To solve this problem I set my base frequency to a very low octave that is not in my music. So, for 432 Hz I would use 27 Hz and for 192 Hz I would use 24 Hz. With these synths I also set the "reference key" to be a very low note that I never actually play. For "A" I use "A0" or "A1" for "G" use "G0" or "G1" etc.

Most of these tuning files including .tun and .scl files are really just text files, and can therefore be edited or even made using a text editor like WordPad. If you make one from scratch, just replace the .txt or other extension with .scl or .tun and it will work just fine.

How to load tuning files in software synths

By now you must really want to know how to load these tuning files into actual synths. I will start with software instruments and then move to hardware. First make a folder somewhere on your PC to keep the tuning files in. Remember where they are so you can browse and easily find them again from your various VST's scale browsers. Each VST is a bit different so I will write instructions for all the ones I have used successfully.

Albino 3®

Just click on the word "Albino" on the bottom right of the synth to see the back. Now, at the bottom right, above the fake stereo out plugs, is a box. Click the load button and browse for the .tun file that you want. Albino comes with some preset .tun files. They will be in your Albino program files (where you installed Albino).

Cronox 2® / CrX4®

Cronox and Crx4 are the same as Albino. Just click on the word "Cronox" or "CrX4" to see the back of the synth, or click "settings" on the top right; it does the same thing. Now browse for your .tun files and load as with Albino, very simple.

Many other Linplug® synths like Octopus® and Spectral® can be micro-tuned and work in the same way as above.

Serum®

Serum works in the same way as Albino and Cronox. Go to the "global" tab and browse for your tuning file from the browser in the oscillator settings. Use the small padlock icon to lock it, then it won't keep going back to equal temperament every time you change sound presets.

Omnisphere 2®

For Omnisphere you have to copy and paste the .tun files into the Omnisphere program files. Just go to:

Program files - spectrasonics - steam - omnisphere - settings library - presets - tuning file

Make a new folder in the "tuning file" folder and call it "my tuning files" (or something like that). Now, just paste your new .tun files into this folder.

To load them, just open Omnisphere and look in the middle of the main front window, a bit to the left. You should see a box called "scale" where you will now find your new folder and files. Use the new "Sound Lock" function and select "tuning scale" to lock the tuning. If you don't it will revert to equal temperament every time you change sound pre-sets.

Alchemy®

As with Omnisphere, go to:

Program files - Camel Audio - alchemy - libraries -tuning

Paste your files in a folder there.

To load them look at the top right of the main window of the synth. There is a box called "Tuning" in which you will now find your .tun files.

Zebra 2®

With Zebra you also need to copy your tuning files into its tuning folder before you can browse for it from the tuning section on the synth. You can find this folder in "my documents" in a folder called "u-he".

Don't forget to toggle "Voice MicroTuning" to "On" (next to the tuning file browser in the synth), as it is off by default. Once it is loaded you can also right click on the file's name in file browser and save it as a preset, then you can load it from there without having to browse for it again. Unfortunately this synth has no tuning lock, and does revert to equal temperament when you change presets.

Kontakt 5®

Kontakt is a great sampler and is perfect sampling your own sounds. It needs a "Kontakt script" to be micro-tuned. In Scala you can save any scale in this format. Just go to "Preferences" - "User Options" - " Synth" and set "Tuning Model" to "129: Native Instruments Kontakt 2, via script file" before exporting your scale.

This script is not an actual tuning file and cannot be loaded directly into Kontakt. To use it you have to open it with a text editor like WordPad, select all of the text (ctrl A), and copy it to your clip board (ctrl C). Now open Kontakt and load any instrument. I don't know why, but this does not work without an instrument loaded. When it is loaded, click the "tuning fork" on the top left of the instrument then click "script editor" on the far right of the instrument window (not the script editor with a scroll icon in the main window). Now, in the row of tabs just below the script editor tab, click on them until you find one that opens an empty white window below it (see following image). If all of the tabs have things in them, try another instrument.

Paste all of the text that is in the Kontakt script file into the empty white space, then hit the "Apply" tab at the top right. Now, to save it go to the "Preset" tab on the left side of the synth, click it and select "save preset" from the drop down menu. Give it a name and save it in the default location, then go to "User" in the same preset tabs drop down menu to see if your file is there. If it is, you will find it there from now on when you browse from any other instrument in Kontakt. In the following image I have highlighted the important tabs in green; this image will help a lot if you have Kontakt open in front of you and don't know where to find everything.

Native synthesizers in Logic®

(EFM1, ESM, ES1, ES2, ESE, ESP, EVB3, EVD6, EVOC 20, EVP88, Garage band Instruments, Sculpture, EXS24).

Logic has very powerful micro-tuning possibilities exclusively for its native synthesizers. It does, however, accept third party VST synthesizers, including the ones in this chapter. So, using .tun files with these that match the .scl files that are tuning the native synthesizers works perfectly. To access the settings for native synthesizers, just go to your "project settings" window and open the "Tuning" section. Here you can change your "software instrument scale" from "equal tempered" to "fixed". When you have done that you can select a scale from the "type" menu (there are already a few scales from the Scala zipfile there). If you want to use you own .scl tuning files, you will need to copy them to your Logic program files so that they appear in the scale type drop down menu in your tuning section.

File path: Pro-app – Contents – Resources – Tuning tables.

Copy your .scl files into the "tuning tables" folder. They should appear in your project settings tuning options. These .scl files don't over-ride your master tune and root key like .tun files do, so you only need one file to play your scale in any key. To change your reference pitch and root key, look in the project tuning settings in Logic.

If you don't have Scala, you can open any of the .scl files that came with Logic and just edit them in a text editor, or just make your own. They work with ratios so you can use any of the ratio based charts in this book to make them. Just make sure that your newly saved files have the .scl extension or they will not work.

Right at the bottom of the tuning options window, you can also select "hermode tuning" which is a self-adapting system that tries to keep your music in just intonation even if you change keys. There are 3 general variations of this that you can choose from: "Baroque" which gives you pure thirds and fifths, "Classic pure" which has slightly tempered thirds and fifths, and "Pop jazz" which has that harmonic seventh that is so important in the overtone series, but can also sound a bit odd at times. The depth slider adjusts the intensity of the tuning in relation to equal temperament. There are a few other settings, too, so I am sure that this system can give good results if set up carefully.

Another nice function is the "copy to user" function on the right of the scale "type" menu. There you can copy the "fixed" scale to the cent based sliders in the "user" section. This is nice if you have a scale where some notes sound a bit off; you can just use your ears to make a quick adjustment. To learn how to use these sliders, read the following Cubase section.

Native synthesizers in Cubase®

As with Logic, Cubase can load all of the VST synthesizers that use .tun files in this chapter, and so it also makes a very good DAW for micro-tuned music. Cubase 7 and later versions also have Hermode tuning which works in the same way as it does in Logic. You can find the settings in "project" – "project setup" (only works with vst 3 synthesizers that are native to CUbase). In older versions of Cubase, most of the native vst 3 synthesizers can also be micro tuned via the Cubase Micro-Tuner plugin. This is a MIDI plugin and must be inserted on a MIDI insert channel, not a regular effect channel. It works in the same way as the "user" scale in Logic, so the following tutorial will work for both programs.

These sliders work with "cents" (percent of 100). You can use the "cents" data from any scale that you have made in Scala, although you do need to make some calculations to get it to work.

With the sliders set to 0 you will have an equal temperament scale with exactly 100 cents in each semi-tone. To calculate the amount of cents needed to shift each note to play the Pythagorean, Ptolemy, or any other scale, just open it in Scala and type "show scale" or go to the "view" tab and select "scale". Then go to "new" - "scale", select equal temperament, open it and do "show scale" again. Now you will be able to see and compare both scales.

You will see your intervals are displayed as cents in the right column. Now all you need to do is look at each note to see if it is higher or lower than the same note in equal temperament. If it is higher you need to raise the cents value, and if it is lower you need to lower it. Remember this "plus or minus" value for each note because it makes the actual calculation much easier.

To complete the calculation, just compare each note to its equal temperament counterpart and subtract the smaller of the two from the larger. The answer that you get will be the amount of cents needed to detune that note from equal temperament to your new scale. Remember to check if the new note is higher or lower than it is in equal temperament, so that you know whether to raise or lower the slider on your micro tuner. You will find that cents don't have the same magical connection to harmonics and numbers that Hz frequencies do. So, when using cents with harmonic intervals, your numbers will usually have many decimals in them and will need to be trimmed.

GOOD TIP: Set your synth to play a single sine or saw tooth wave with no effects or modulation, and then use the "tuner" plugin in Cubase® or a similar Hz based guitar tuner to check that you really have the right frequencies.

How to load tuning files in hardware synths

For hardware synths you need to export your scale from Scala in the correct format for that synth. Only some hardware synths can be micro tuned like this, and you will definitely need your synth's operation manual to find out the specifics for each synth, like the strange key combinations sometimes needed to activate midi dumps. Some modern synths also have a usb port that can load tuning files, usually using a specific format and loading method for that synth.

Many hardware synths use some form of bulk dump midi files. Scala can make quite a few types of these midi files, so if you have the right synth and want to load one of these files into it, all you need to do is follow these steps.

Loading midi dump files:

1. Load your midi dump file on a midi track in your music workstation (Cubase® Logic® etc.) or hardware sequencer.

2. Connect the "MIDI Out" of your workstation to the "MIDI In" of your hardware synth.

3. Solo the Track with the midi file and make sure your synth and computer are set to the same midi channel (channel 1 is best as it is often the default setting).

4. Make sure your hardware synth is set up to receive a bulk midi dump (this info you will find in your synths user manual).

5. Play back the data into your synth by hitting the play button in your workstation. Wait until it is played through and this should do it. Your synth "will" now be re-tuned.

Here is a fairly complete list of hardware and software synths that are compatible with Scala.

(List from the Scala website)

Alphakanal Automat

AnaMark softsynth

Big Tick Angelina, Rainbow and Rhino softsynths

Bitheadz Unity softsynth

Cakewalk Dimension Pro

Cakewalk Rapture

Cakewalk Z3ta+ softsynth

Camel Audio Alchemy and Cameleon5000 softsynths

Celemony Melodyne 2

ChucK

crusherX-Mac!

DashSignature EVE one (not two)

Devine Machine OTR88

E-mu Morpheus

E-mu Proteus series

Ensoniq EPS/EPS16/ASR10

Ensoniq TS-10/TS-12

Fluidsynth (iiwusynth) software synthesizer

HERCs series, Abakos Pro softsynths

Image-Line Harmor

Kemper Digital Virus

Korg M1, M1R octave tuning dump

Korg X5DR octave tuning dump

Korg OASYS PCI soundcard (and softsynths supporting its .tun tuning textfile)

LinPlug Albino 2, Alpha 2, CronoX, Octopus, Organ 3 and Sophistry softsynths

Manytone ManyStation, ManyGuitar, ManyOne softsynths

Marion MSR-2

Max Magic Microtuner for Max/MSP and Pluggo softsynths

MIDI Tuning Standard (both bulk tuning dump and single-note tuning change, 3 byte), supported in Timidity and Audio Compositor, E-mu: Proteus 3, UltraProteus, Audity/Proteus

1000 and 2000 series, Virtuoso 2000, Proteus FX, Orbit, Planet Phatt, B3, Carnaval, Ensoniq: ASR-X, MR Rack, MR-61, MR-76, ZR-76, Turtle Beach: Multisound, Monterey, Maui, Tropez, Rio

MIDI Tuning Standard 2-byte octave tuning dump

MIDI Tuning Standard 1-byte octave tuning dump

MIDI to CSound

Modartt Pianoteq 4

Mutagene Mukoco, Macomate 88

Moog Slim Phatty. (Latest model, 100% analogue hardware synth, uses .scl files)

Omringen Oblivion

Native Instruments Absynth 2 (via .gly file)

Native Instruments FM7 and Pro-52/Pro-53

Native Instruments Kontakt 2 (via script file)

Native Instruments Reaktor (via semitones file, frequency file or NTF file)

Pure Data

Robin Schmidt's Straightliner softsynth

Roland GS & JV/XP families

Roland Fantom-X6/X7/X8

Roland V-Synth Version 2.0

Roland Virtual Sound Canvas, SC-8850

Smart Electronix Foorius

Spectrasonics Omnisphere softsynth

Synapse Audio Orion Pro softsynth

Synthesis Technology MOTM-650

Synthogy Ivory

Timidity and Audio Compositor MIDI to audio renderers

Tobybear Helios softsynth

VAZ Plus, 2001 and Modular softsynths VirSyn Cube, Cantor, Poseidon and TERA 2 softsynths

Xponaut Voice Tweaker

Yamaha DX7II/TX802. Classic digital hardware synths.

Yamaha SY77/TG77/SY99/VL-1/VL-7

Yamaha TX81Z/DX11/DX27/DX100/V50 (both octave and full keyboard bulk data)

Yamaha XG family

Yamaha VL70m

WayOutWare TimewARP 2600

Wusik Wusikstation v2

Xenharmonic FMTS VSTi

Zebra 2.0 softsynth

Tuning acoustic instruments

If you are tuning an actual instrument like a harp, then your best bet will be to look at the charts in this book or generate frequency charts yourself in Scala. Then you could use a hardware or software Hz reading tuner and a microphone to tune your instrument. Another very good way is to use a VST synth with your scale loaded and with a pure sine or saw wave preset, and then tune the actual instrument to match the notes by ear. It is also good to know that there are many Pythagorean 432 Hz, 256 Hz, 192 Hz and 288 Hz tuning forks available online. These are great for tuning instruments by ear.

Brainwave entrainment techniques

Brainwave states		
8 High gamma	64 - 128 Hz	Self-awareness, unity, super-conscious, deep insight, healing.
7 Gamma	32 - 64 Hz	Highly alert, insight, information processing, hyperactivity.
6 Beta	16 - 32 Hz	Alert, normal waking state, concentration, critical thought.
5 Alpha	8 - 16 Hz	Calm, daydreaming, visualization, memory, serotonin release.
4 Theta	4 - 8 Hz	Lucid dreaming, hallucinogenic state, intuition.
3 Delta	2 – 4 Hz	Transcendental meditation, sleep, natural opiate release.
2 Low delta	1 – 2 Hz	Deep meditation, deep sleep, endorphin release, healing.
1 Epsilon	0 – 1 Hz	Insight, self-awareness, unity, universal mind, deep healing.

Binaural beats

Binaural beats are most often made using software, although you can use acoustic instruments, too. In ancient times people used two de-tuned singing bowls, didgeridoos, or other drone producing instruments. Nowadays, however, there is some very nice software available for creating binaural beats. As usual the most useful software is freeware / shareware that not many people know about, like "Valhalla echo®". If you want to make binaural beats using your DAW, then this simple little plugin is a gem.

Valhalla echo®

"Valhalla echo®" can be downloaded here for free: http://www.valhalladsp.com/valhallafreqecho. To install it simply unzip the file to the directory where you normally install your effect plugins.

While it is really meant for making crazy sounds, it can also be used to de-tune left /right channels to specific Hz and so can be used to de-tune any sounds, making them into binaural beats. This is very useful because pure computer-generated sine waves can be rather harsh. With this plugin, however, you can use a warm analogue sine wave or any sound that you want to be your carrier signal.

When all the knobs are set up just as they are in this image (make sure "delay sync" is set to "free") then the big middle knob becomes a stereo Hz de-tuner. This is very useful because it is a plugin, and so can be used in real time on any sound in a full song. It is particularly nice to set up an FX send channel with a reverb and Valhalla echo after it, then you can send this to many channels creating a nice ambient / binaural wash in the background through your whole track (a group track can be set up in a similar way).

If you use harmonic bpm then this is a powerful tool. Just divide your bpm by 60 and use octaves of that frequency to dial into Valhalla. The slider is too sensitive for exact Hz work, but you can click on the numbers under the dial (Hz) and enter any frequency with your PC keyboard. You can also right click on the numbers and use "copy and paste" to paste numbers from your calculator or a text file, which is very handy.

You should note that if the dial is set to 4 Hz, it raises the right channel by 4 Hz and also lowers the left by 4 Hz. So, with a setting of 4 Hz, the end binaural beat will be 8 Hz and not 4 Hz. The fact that it raises and lowers both channels is good because this makes it more musically useful. If it only lowered one channel then the resulting sound would be a bit flat, whereas if it raised one channel then it would be a bit sharp. All in all, this is pretty much the best tool that I have found for adding binaural beats into music.

BWGEN®

Brainwave generator or BWGEN is another amazing piece of software downloadable for free here: http://www.bwgen.com/download.htm

It is stand-alone (not a plugin) but it does have an "export to wave file" option. With BWGEN you can easily make the classic sine wave based binaural beats that you see on YouTube, or buy online as products with names like "E dose". It can produce triangle, square, and other useful wave forms, and can also have more than one binaural beat at the same time. So, it can be used to create more complex brain states.

BWGEN comes with some nice presets that you can use or edit as a starting point. You can easily make your own from scratch, too.

Here is a quick lesson:

Go to "wave" and then "preset options" and "general" to open the user options window. Here you can name your program, set its length in minutes, and add segments and voices. Segments are for more complex changes in your program, while voices are for adding more than one voice or tone at the same time.

Now go to "sound" next to "general". Here can set your binaural beat frequency and your audible pitch frequency. If you have more than one voice you need to go back to "general" and "voices" and select each voice to edit them there.

Your tones can easily be set to sweep from one frequency to another. Just click on the small square white "nodes" to open the "sweep parameters" box. The default setting for the audible pitch is to track the binaural beat frequency; that generates an audible pitch that is in mathematical harmony with the binaural beat frequency. This is helpful if your binaural beat frequency is slowly changing over time, and you still want a harmonious tone for a carrier that changes in harmony with moving beat frequency. If you want to set your own frequency, uncheck this "track" box and use the small square white "nodes" to open the "sweep parameters" box. Then you can set a stable or sweeping frequency for your carrier voice. With a stable Hz frequency for the carrier tone you can make sounds that are in tune with your music's root frequency.

The next preset option next to "sound" is "waveform" where you can choose different waveforms for each voice. This is quite nice because with the square and triangle waves you can also make crazy short binaural sound effects. In the other two boxes, "background" and "noise", you can set up background sounds to mix with the beats, such as nature sounds, white / pink noise etc. I would really recommend adding sounds in a better audio workstation, though. To do this just export your binaural beats to wave under "wave" and "play into .WAV file", then load them into your workstation.

Cool edit pro®

Adobe® Cool edit pro also has a nice brainwave synchronizer under "effects" and "special" called "brainwave synchronizer". This is a nice and very simple way to apply binaural de-tuning to any audio.

Isochronic tones

A scientific isochronic tone is a very carefully shaped and tuned sound. The best way to make pure isochronic tones is in your PC music workstation; for example, in Cubase or Logic. If you want to make pure "scientific" tones with no music, a very interesting option is to set your quantize to seconds instead of beats and bars (I have only done this in Cubase). When you do this it disables your normal quantize and enables the other milliseconds (ms) quantize next to it. Now you don't need to worry about Hz / bpm conversion. I have tried to make normal music like this (using only seconds and milliseconds) but it is quite tricky. Using bpm and normal quantize is more familiar.

There are two ways to get your actual tones. You can just use a synth with a pure wave form, or you can make the waves in another program and import them as audio. If you render them first, it is good to render them a bit longer than they should be, because then you can edit out start or end clicks to make nice clean pulses. This way you can also line all of the wave shapes up better, by always starting on a "zero point" in the center where the wave crosses the line of no air pressure. Another method is to use long waves with a gate effect to create the isochronic pulse.

When you work with isochronic tones the border between brainwave work and music becomes really thin. For example, one known way of working with isochronic tones is to apply a randomizer to the carrier tones frequency and / or panning so that each successive tone is a different random frequency or in a different ear. Music producers do this all the time. It is just one step away from being a panned melody or arpeggiated synth line, very much like the African tribes who use those stereo interlocking "binaural" melodies to induce trance by placing an mbira player at each ear of the trancer.

If you tune your music to its harmonic bpm, then your music will automatically be isochronic. All you really need to do is study this chart and keep in mind what kind of rhythms create which kind of brainwave, knowing that the rules are the same for any bpm between 120 and 240 bpm.

Brainwave	Sound example	Quantize	Bpm
Epsilon	Quarter time	1/1	120 to 240
Low delta	Half time snr-drum	1/2	120 to 240
Delta	Straight trance kick	1/4	120 to 240
Theta	Double time hi-hat	1/8	120 to 240
Alpha	Kbbb kick-bass	1/16	120 to 240
Beta	Drum roll	1/32	120 to 240
Gamma	Very low C bass	1/64	120 to 240
High gamma	C bass	1/128	120 to 240

Embedding brainwaves into pre-made music

There are many ways to go about this. One of my favorites is to split my audio into frequency bands using equalizers or filters, and then apply binaural de-tuning, isochronic gating or even just mild amplitude modulation or panning to one or more of these bands. The best software to use for this is your normal DAW such as Cubase or Logic. You do get special software for de-tuning audio and embedding beats, but they are all very limited and will never be as good as a workstation with all its equalizers and filters.

Separating your music into frequency bands is actually quite simple. If, for example, you want to separate the sub bass from some music so that you can de-tune it without affecting the higher parts, all you need to do is duplicate your song channel so you have two channels with the same thing playing:

Then just apply different equalizers to each channel, so one channel will play only bass while the other plays only mid-range and high frequencies:

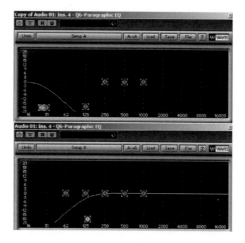

Now all you need to do is apply isochronic gating, binaural detuning or other forms of modulation to the channel that is playing only bass. Obviously if you want to embed binaural beats, just use Valhalla delay on the bass track. Of course you can use other frequency ranges in narrow bands, not only sub bass and not only 2 frequencies. For more frequencies just open another channel and use another EQ to isolate another frequency band.

iZotope Spectron ®

There is a very nice plugin for separating frequencies into narrow bands in this way. It is called "iZotope Spectron ®". With this plugin you can solo or bypass any frequency band (see small square solo / bypass check boxes in image below). If you solo a band as I have in the image below, then it will play only that band. And if you bypass that band it will play everything but that band.

So, all you need to do is put a Spectron with identical settings on each of your 2 channels that are both playing the same song, and set one to solo and the other one to bypass. Now, when you play both channels together your song will sound whole again, and you will be able to apply some Valhalla delay (binaural detune), some isochronic gating or other tempo synch effects to the channel with the soloed Spectron.

In this way your binaural beats or other modulation will only be applied to a narrow band of frequencies, leaving the rest of the song unaffected. You also don't have to only use 2 bands, you could cut out more frequencies on the channel set to "bypass". Then you just need to add another audio channel playing the whole song with another Spectron soloing that same frequency. With this method you could embed many different binaural frequencies into the same song, or you could have combinations of different entrainment methods on different bands. If you study the picture above you can quickly set Spectron up in exactly the same way without reading the very long manual.

Just remember that if you want it to sound really good and to be healthy, you should find out what bpm the music you are using has. Then you can use frequencies and pulses that are in harmony with it (see the chapter Harmonic bpm). Apart from being more harmonious for your brain and not giving you a headache, if there are audible pulses or de-tune wobbles they will still sound musically good as they will be in time with the music.

Subliminal audio

Subliminal sounds are sounds that are hidden either just below or above hearing range, at a very low volume behind louder sounds, or masked in some other way. If you want to make subliminal binaural beats or isochronic tones, a good way is to simply use audio frequencies for your tones that are just above or below our hearing range but still within the range of audio equipment. You could use the same method of band separation for embedding audio into pre-made music to do this. Or, if you are a producer, you can just add subliminal sounds to your music while you are making it.

Subliminal messages

I never use these because the way they work is by by-passing your conscious mind, the part that makes decisions like "this message is bullshit", and it goes directly to your subconscious. If you do make audio with subliminal messages, remember that you will be the first to be programmed while trying to make it. So, generally I would advise against using hidden words or messages, even "positive" ones. If you really have to do it, though, you could use a vocoder with a carrier frequency that is just out of hearing range, and your secret message voice as the modulator.

Another way is to record a very long file with your message repeating over and over again, then pitch shift this file so that it becomes a tone that is just above human hearing range. If you use harmonic bpm for this, you can make a tone that is within hearing range and also in tune with your music; basically, nice FM sounds made from repeating words...

Just be careful; taking away a person's and your own choice to think independent thoughts might not be the best thing for you to do even if you think you know what they / you should be thinking.

Subliminal sounds

Examples of less scary subliminal sounds would be to have subliminally soft recordings of forests and other nature sounds hidden in your music, very low isochronic tones or binaural beats to add subsonic subconscious harmony to your sounds and such things. Some say that your subconscious mind can decode backward sounds, sounds that are sped up or slowed down a lot and even randomized. So, the possibilities of subliminal sound are really as big as your imagination.

Primal sound

Primal sound is another healthy side of this kind of thing. Primal sounds are a type of subliminal sound where you take a recording of nature, a person's heartbeat or other sound, pitch shift it to a much higher or lower pitch, or even use other effects to change them into different sounds. The resulting sounds are always familiar and can bring up primal memories. I use these all the time in my music by making small birds into giant dinosaurs and things like that.

Good software for pitch shifting is Sound Forge® because of its "do not preserve duration" option. This also slows the track down as it stretches it out, making it longer but keeping the harmonic intervals etc. the same as if you were physically slowing a record or tape down. Just make sure to un-check that "preserve duration" box if you want clean sounds with no noisy digital sound artifacts. The free-ware "Audacity" also works for this. Just use the "change speed" effect (it changes the speed and pitch together) and not the pitch shift one.

The end...

I am putting a course together in which you will be able to hear everything in this book as audio files, and I'm also working on a micro-tuning course for producers. For updates on this, more info, help or free tuning files, join my Facebook Group "Life, the Universe and 432 Hz" and change the group settings so that you actually get updates. If you want to be on my e-mail list, the best way is to "buy" one of the free songs on my indigo aura band camp page and add your e-mail there.

Links

Micro-tuned music:

Ambient meditation: https://indigoaura.bandcamp.com/

Forest trance: https://soundcloud.com/psychederic

Main website: http://mathemagicalmusic.weebly.com/

FB group: https://www.facebook.com/groups/345636055517218/

Made in the USA
Middletown, DE
19 July 2017